REIHE CANTZ

ULRIKE FLAIG

SOUNDCHECK

INSTALLATIONEN / INSTALLATIONS

INHALT *CONTENTS*

Mit größer werdender Distanz gewinnen ihre Bilder an Deutlichkeit. Das ist ein überraschender und – angesichts ihrer Materialintensität – nicht unmittelbar einleuchtender Befund im Hinblick auf die künstlerische Arbeit von Ulrike Flaig, der in seinen Teilen zu präzisieren ist. Was meint ›Bild‹, was ›Distanz‹ und was ›Deutlichkeit‹?

Ulrike Flaig arbeitet mit einem sehr weiten Bildbegriff, gewissermaßen einem nach innen wie nach außen stark erweiterten Umriss von Bildlichkeit. Das ist an ihrer Arbeit ›Die Tapferkeit oder das Stärkersein als man selbst‹ (1997), die nicht zufällig in dieser Publikation breiten Raum einnimmt, besonders eindringlich zu beobachten. Zunächst ist da die einer provisorischen Unterkunft ähnelnde Raumkonstruktion, deren Begrenzungen aus weißem Plexiglas und Folien, auf welchen sich die Objekte im Inneren abzeichnen, eine erste Ebene sowohl plastisch wie abstrakt lesbarer Bildlichkeit entwickeln. Die physische Präsenz dieser ›Raum-Bilder‹ wird auf einer nächsten Ebene unterwandert von virtuell erzeugten Bildern der Oberfläche und des nicht einsehbaren Inneren des gebauten Bildraumes. In der Fantasie des Betrachters beginnen die virtuellen Bilder die Stelle der ›wirklichen‹ Bilder einzunehmen, mit dem Ergebnis, das wir uns gedanklich aus dem gegebenen Raum des materialen Kunstobjekts immer weiter herausbewegen: Die Inversion von Bildlichkeit – im Sinne von Umkehrung, Umwandlung und Einstülpung – führt den Betrachter zu einer introspektiven Bilderkenntnis.

Damit ist der für das Verständnis der Arbeit von Ulrike Flaig wesentliche Begriff der Distanz und der Distanzierung ins Spiel gebracht. Ihr nur vordergründig spielerisch-anarchisch anmutender, tatsächlich mit kühlem Kopf entwickelter Materialmix und die offen zur Schau gestellte Unzuverlässigkeit ihrer Objekte – was ihre Belastbarkeit und ihre Lebensdauer betrifft – entspringen im Grunde einer raffinierten Strategie, mit welcher der Betrachter sowohl physisch wie mental auf Distanz gebracht wird. Je weiter ich zurücktrete, desto deutlicher nimmt Gestalt an, was aus der Nähe nur abstrakte Konfiguration war. Will heißen: Je weniger ich Deutung und Bedeutung im Objekt suche, stattdessen meine erinnerten Bilder mit dem offenen Bildangebot der künstlerischen Konzeption zusammenschließe, umso deutlicher formt sich das Ganze einer ›Erzählung‹, welche Momente der eigenen Biografie gegenständlich erfasst, bearbeitet, verwandelt und weiterschreibt. ›Erzählerisch‹ strukturiert ist daher auch die vorliegende

Publikation, welche die körperliche und geistige Begegnung des Betrachters mit dem Werk – vom Close-up bis zur Vogelperspektive, von der Identifizierung einer Materialbeschaffenheit bis zum frei fantasierenden Weiterspinnen des Bildangebots – zu antizipieren sucht. Ihre Eindringlichkeit gewinnen Flaigs Objekte und Installationen aber daraus, dass sie das Thema der Erinnerung aus einer distanzierteren Haltung anschaulich werden lassen und damit in einem nicht persönlichen, allgemeineren Sinne psychologische, gesellschaftliche und politische Aspekte einräumen.

RENATE WIEHAGER PREFACE

Ulrike Flaig's images become more distinct as the distance increases. This is a surprising and, in light of the material intensity, not an altogether self-evident fact about her oeuvre, and it needs some explanation. What is meant by ›image‹, by ›distance‹, and by ›clarity‹?
Ulrike Flaig works with a rather broad concept of the image, an outline of the pictorial, so-to-speak, greatly extended both towards the inside and outside. Her work ›Braveness or Being Stronger than Oneself‹ (1997), which – no mere coincidence – is also prominently featured in this publication, constitutes a prime example. First, there is the spatial construction resembling a temporary shelter. Its boundaries of white Plexiglas and foil – through which the objects inside are barely discernible – present a first layer of imagery, legible both in a sculptural and abstract sense. On the next level, the physical presence of these ›spatial images‹ is suffused with virtual images of surface and of the hidden interior of the constructed pictorial space. In the imagination of the viewer, virtual images soon replace the ›real‹, and, as a result, our thoughts begin to roam further and further beyond the given space of the material art object: the inversion of the pictorial – the reversal, transformation and turning inward that is – guides the viewer to an introspective comprehension of the image.
Thus, we have arrived at distance and distancing – two terms so essential for the understanding of Ulrike Flaig's works. Her mix of materials is only at first glance playfully anarchistic, in reality, it derives from level-headed calculation. This and the openly displayed unreliability of her objects, both with respect to durability and wear, are actually part of a sophisticated strategy keeping the viewer at a distance, mentally and physically. The more I step back, the clearer the shape of what seemed only an abstract configu-

ration close up. Or: the less I am looking for interpretation and meaning in the object, joining the images remembered with the images offered up by artistic conception instead, the more clearly the whole melds into a ›narrative‹ representing moments of my own biography, processing, transforming and continuing them. Appropriately, this publication also follows a ›narrative‹ path in its attempt to anticipate the physical and mental encounter of viewer and work – from the close-up to the bird's-eye view, from identifying material texture to letting the imagination run free beyond the image displayed. And yet, Flaig's objects and installations gain their sense of urgency from the fact that they illustrate the topic of remembrance from a more distanced point-of-view, thus admitting psychological, social and political aspects not in a personal, but in a more general sense.

BEAT WYSS WO STECKT HIER KUNST?

Etwa in den abgebildeten Dingen? Aber warum erscheinen sie denn so verhuscht in der Wiedergabe?

Aha – das Spiel von Licht und Schatten … ist es etwa das? Die Künstlerin verzaubert den Kunstraum in ein eigenartig bevölkertes Terrarium. Oder scheint das nur so, vermittelt über die Fotografie?

Die Fotografie! Steckt darin die Kunst? Aber was zeigt diese denn anderes als verhuschte Dinge und Spiele von Licht und Schatten? Wir drehen uns im Kreis.

Steckt Kunst gar im Katalog, der uns zeigt, dass das alles zusammenwirkt? Was wir auf diesen Buchseiten sehen, sind Momentaufnahmen von sichtbaren Dingen auf dem Weg zum Betrachter.

In der alten Kunst waren die technischen Verfahren Mittel zum Zweck. Bildhauerische Techniken und Kniffe, Methoden der Farbmischung waren bestgehütetes Geheimnis der Meisterwerkstatt und hatten für die Aussage selbst nichts zu bedeuten. Es ging um die Erscheinung an Inhalten, die das Werk auszustrahlen hatte; allenfalls stellte die Sichtbarkeit des Verfahrens den virtuosen Umgang des Schöpfers mit seinen technischen Mitteln unter Beweis. Seit dem Popzeitalter jedoch wird das Verfahren selbst zum Inhalt der Kunst – nach Marshall McLuhans allbekanntem Satz: ›Das Medium ist die Botschaft.‹

Am Kunstfoto interessiert nicht das Dargestellte, sondern die körnige Struktur; am Kunstvideo der Flimmereffekt und die kontingente Verwischung; am digitalen Kunstbild der Reiz des Unwahrscheinlichen in der naturgetreuen Simulation.

Alle gegenwärtigen Verfahren lassen sich auf einen Nenner bringen: Kunstproduktion besteht im uneigentlichen Gebrauch von Technologie. Künstler sind Anwender von Material, das nicht für ihre Arbeit erfunden wurde.

Das Logo der Künstlerin: zwei Turnschuhe und ein weißer Ball mit der Aufschrift ›Mobiler-Meister-Service‹. Ulrike Flaig leitet einen Ding-Zirkus. Zu den Darstellern gehören: Monitoren, Projektoren, Ventilatoren; Videobeamer und Luftballone; Glühbirnen und Neon, viel elektrisches Kabel; Stuhl und Tisch, aber nicht zum Draufsitzen. Nur der Feuerlöscher gehört zur Einrichtung der Galerie – für den Fall. Ferner wirken mit: Polyester, Styropor, Nylon, Gummi, Holz, Glasfaser und Plexiglas.

All das Gewimmel ist arrangiert, um zu erzeugen, was John Dewey ›eine Erfahrung‹ nennt. Während wir beim gewöhnlichen Wahrnehmen pausenlos von Signalen umtost werden, aus denen wir die uns nützlichen Informationen herausfiltern müssen, wird in der Wahrnehmung von Kunst diese Überfülle verlangsamt, verfremdet oder ganz stillgelegt. Ästhetische Erfahrung kommt durch eine Verknappung der Sinnenreize zustande. Das Anhalten von Wahrnehmung gibt uns Aufschluss über die Natur des Wahrnehmens. Ihres Zwecks entkleidet, werden Zeichen als Zeichen erkennbar und prüfbar in ihrer Wirkung auf uns.
Das Ethos der Kunst besteht in der Unterbrechung von Praxis: dieser Bedingung der Möglichkeit nachzudenken.

Dass Kunst ein Ding ist, das sich erst im Netzwerk der Vermittlung entfaltet, geht auf Minimal und Concept Art zurück. Nun gibt sich Ulrike Flaig nicht so knapp und wortkarg wie etwa Don Judd. Schon in ihren Titeln zeigt sie sich gesprächig und erst recht in den Objekten: Da surrt es, dreht sich's und blinkt und verbreitet eine Poesie und Heiterkeit, die an den Nouveau Réalisme der späten fünfziger Jahre erinnert.
Dabei sollte man diese Arbeiten – zwar aus zweckentfremdetem Gerät und industriellem Material gezimmert – nicht vorschnell mit dem Absurden bei Jean Tinguely verbinden. Das Fabulierende bei Ulrike Flaig hat weder mit Neo-Dada noch Surrealismus zu tun. Ihre Kunst führt vor, wie sie selber zustande kommt. Sie zeigt, was es da zu reden gibt, wenn die Dinge und das Publikum sich in der Galerie begegnen. Von ferne, auf dem Seziertisch, mögen Lautréamonts Regenschirm und Nähmaschine zufällig grüßen; doch die Ironie von Ulrike Flaig steht der von Artschwager näher.
Diese Kunst ist Kommunikation im absoluten Modellfall. Ulrike Flaig schlägt als Regisseurin der Wahrnehmung den Betrachtern Sichtweisen vor, die über Text, Fotografie und Film belegt werden. Die Vermittlung ist Bestandteil der Kunst. Ob es diesem Text gelungen ist, sich an das Drehbuch zu halten?

BEAT WYSS WHERE IS THE ART HERE?

Perhaps in the things that are shown? But why do they appear so vague, so blurred?

Aha, the play of light and shadow … maybe it's that – the artist magically turning the space into a strangely populated terrarium. Or does it only seem that way, due to the photography?

The photography! Is that where the art is? But what does it show apart from blurred things and the play of light and shadow? We are obviously going around in circles.

Well, maybe there is art in the catalogue, showing us how all this fits together? What we see on these pages, after all, are momentary records of visible things on their way to the observer.

In earlier art, the technical processes were a means to an end. Sculptural techniques and tricks of the trade, ways of mixing colours were the master workshops' well-kept secrets and had no meaning for the actual expression itself. The content that the work was meant to convey was all that was important; evidence of artistic processes at the most served to display the artist's obvious mastery of the tools of his trade. Yet, ever since the pop age, the process itself has become the content of art – in Marshall McLuhan's well-known words: ›The medium is the message‹.

In an art photo, it is not the thing represented that is of interest, rather, the grainy structure; in an art video, it is the contingent effect of flickering and blurring, in the digital art image, the charm of something improbable in a true-to-life simulation.

All contemporary processes can be brought to a common denominator: art production consists of an unseemly use of technology. Artists are users of material that wasn't invented for their work.

The logo of the artist: two gym shoes and a white ball with the motto ›Mobile Master Service‹. Ulrike Flaig is the director of a ›thing-circus‹. Among the performers are: monitors, projectors, fans; video projectors and balloons; light bulbs and neon, masses of electrical cable; chair and table, but not for sitting. Only the fire extinguisher is part of the gallery – just in case. Polyester, Styro-foam, nylon, rubber, wood, fibreglass and Plexiglas play supporting roles.

The whole jumble is arranged in order to create what John Dewey calls ›an experience‹. Normally, our perceptions are buzzing with signals, and from these, we have to filter the information that is useful to us. In the perception of art, this overload is slowed down, distorted or brought to a complete halt. Aesthetic experience is achieved by reducing sensory stimulus. Interrupting the perception process provides us with information about the nature of perception. Stripped of their purpose, signs become recognizable as signs, and their effect on us may be analysed.

The ethos of art consists in the interruption of standard practice, the very condition for the possibility of reflection.

The idea that art is something which only reveals itself in the context of its transmission goes back to Minimal and Concept Art. Yet, Ulrike Flaig is certainly not as taciturn and unconversational as, for example, Don Judd. She is talkative even in her titles, and more so in her objects: things hum, rotate and flash, dispensing a poetry and mirth that recall the Nouveau Réalisme of the late Fifties.

Even so, one should not prematurely connect these works – although cobbled together from industrial materials and devices alienated from their purposes – with the absurd art of Jean Tinguely. Ulrike Flaig's narrative streak is neither related to the Neo-Dada nor to Surrealism. Her art celebrates its coming about. It actually shows what there is to talk about when the things and the public meet in the gallery. From a distance, on the dissecting table, Lautréamont's umbrella and sewing machine might send a greeting; but Ulrike Flaig's irony is closer to that of Artschwager.

This kind of art is a model of communication in the extreme. Ulrike Flaig, as the director of the viewers' perceptions, suggests ways of seeing via text, photography and film. The transmission is an integral part of the art. Has this text managed to stick to the script?

DIE TAPFERKEIT ODER
DAS STÄRKERSEIN ALS MAN SELBST

1997 *BRAVENESS OR BEING STRONGER THAN ONESELF*

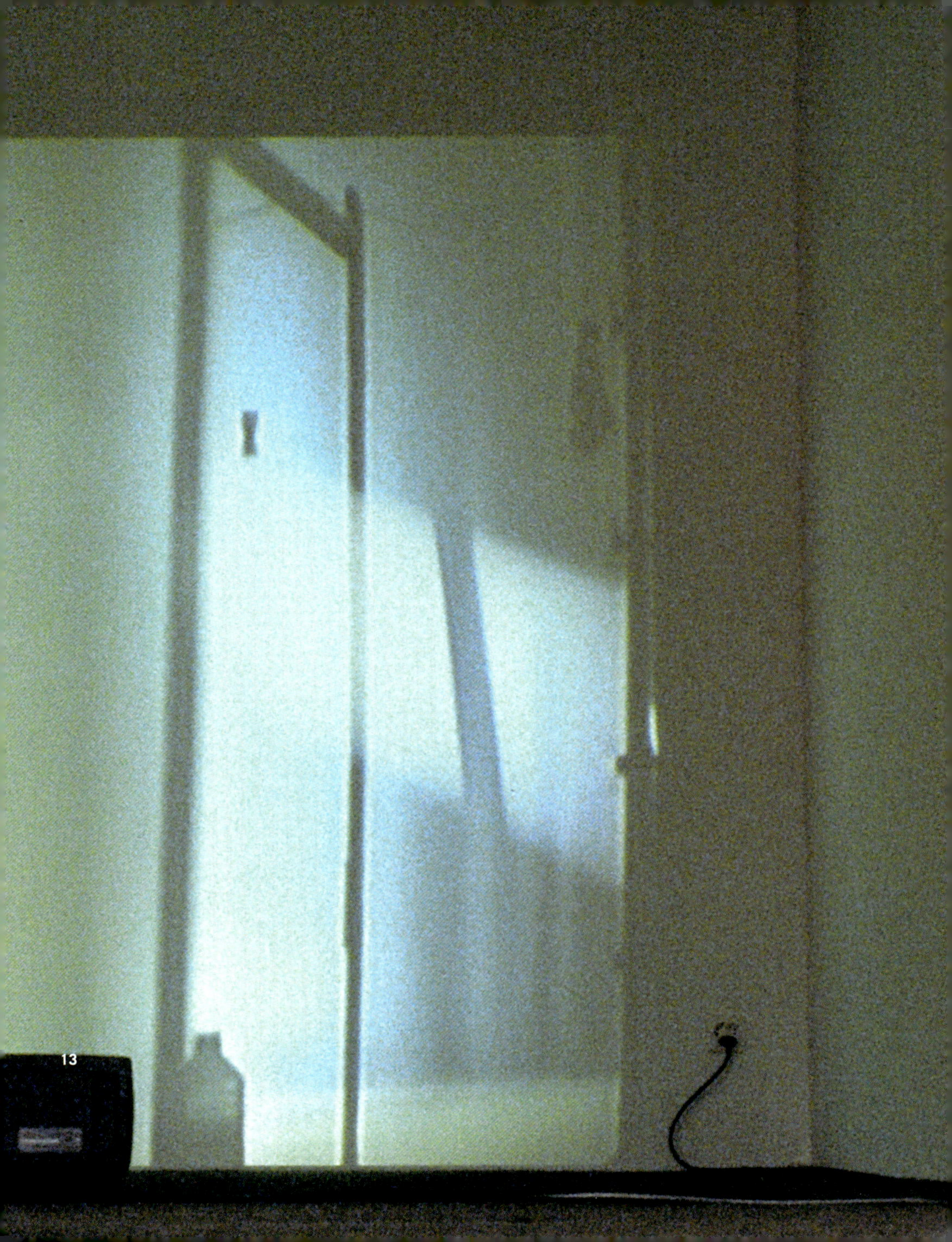
13

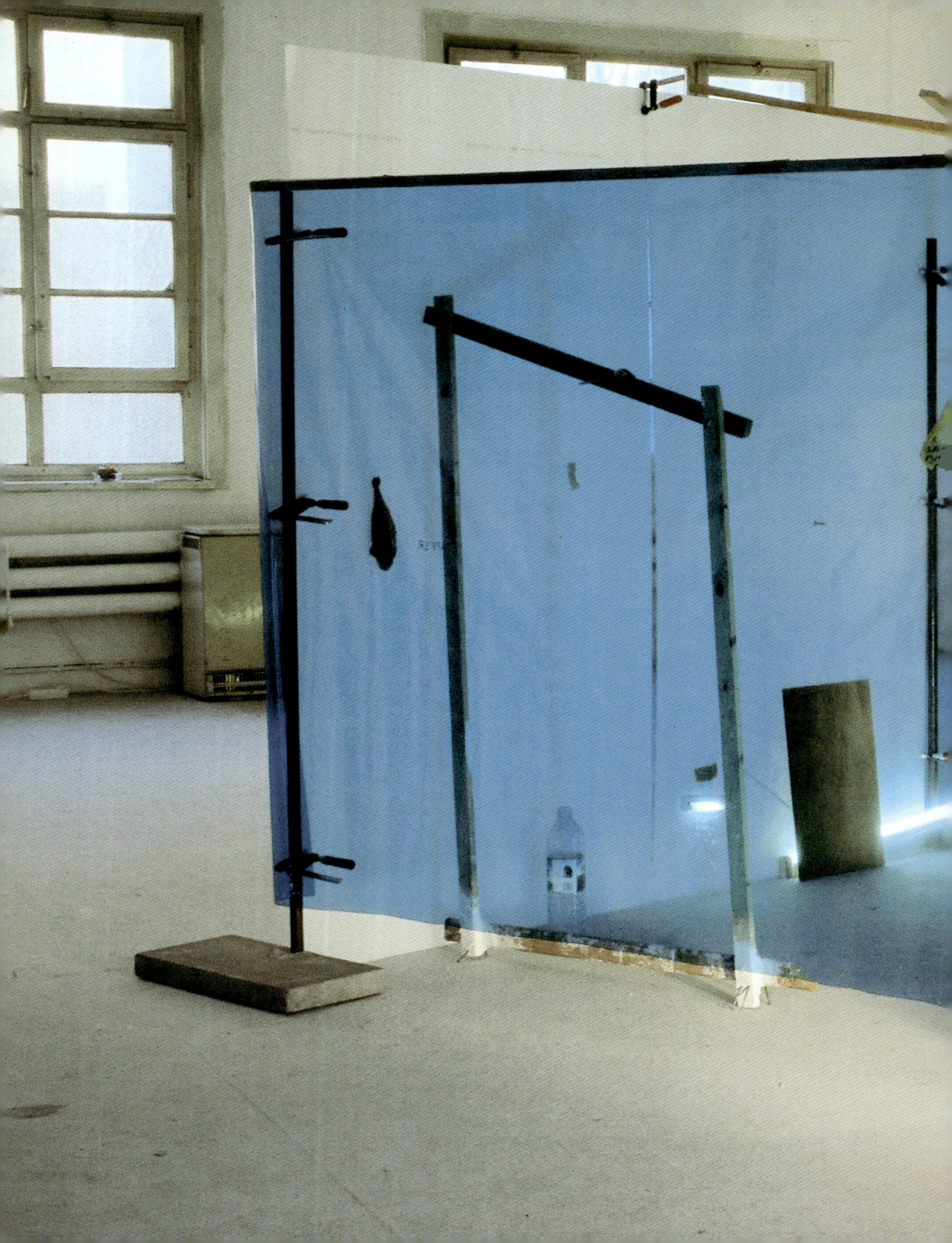

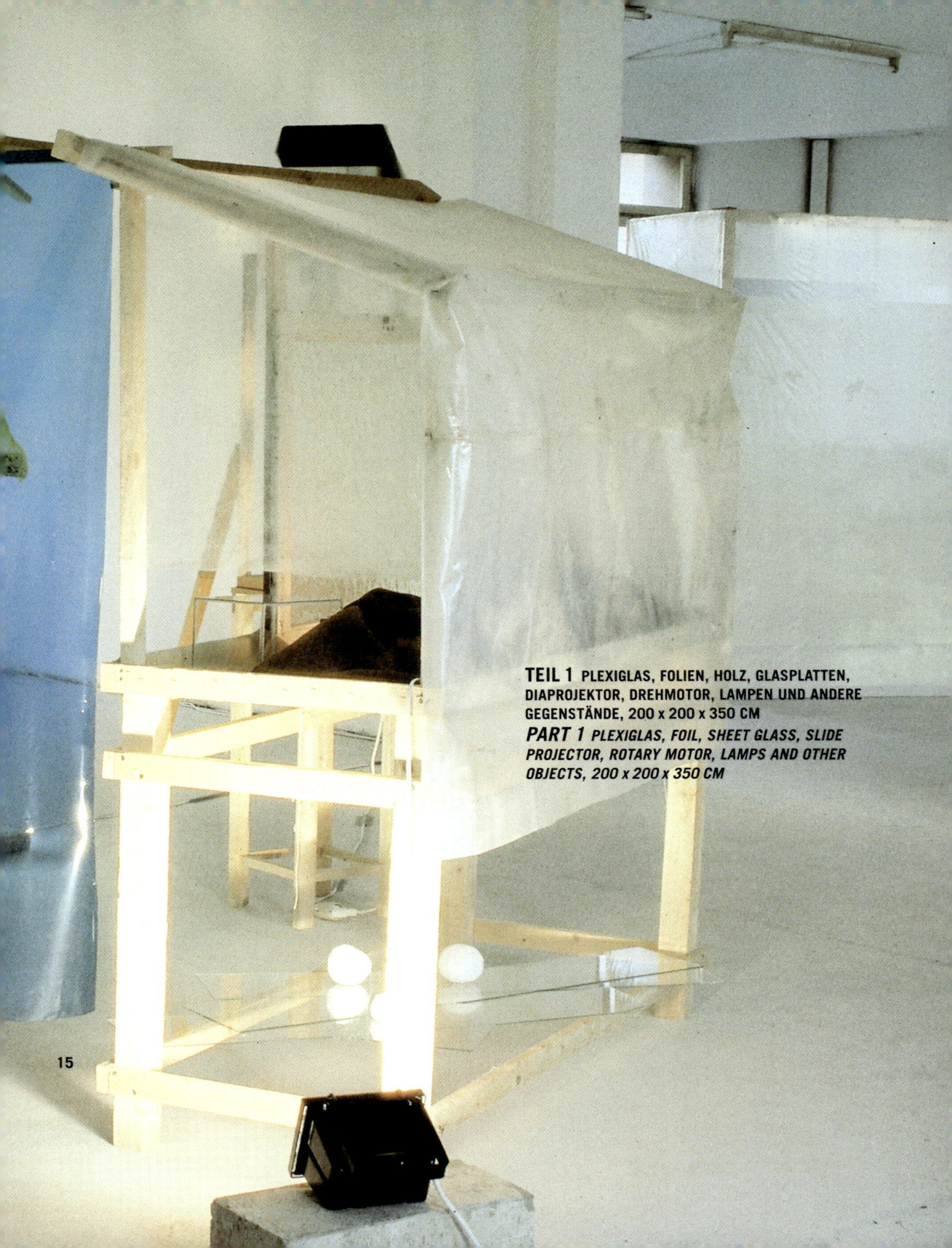

TEIL 1 PLEXIGLAS, FOLIEN, HOLZ, GLASPLATTEN,
DIAPROJEKTOR, DREHMOTOR, LAMPEN UND ANDERE
GEGENSTÄNDE, 200 x 200 x 350 CM
PART 1 PLEXIGLAS, FOIL, SHEET GLASS, SLIDE
PROJECTOR, ROTARY MOTOR, LAMPS AND OTHER
OBJECTS, 200 x 200 x 350 CM

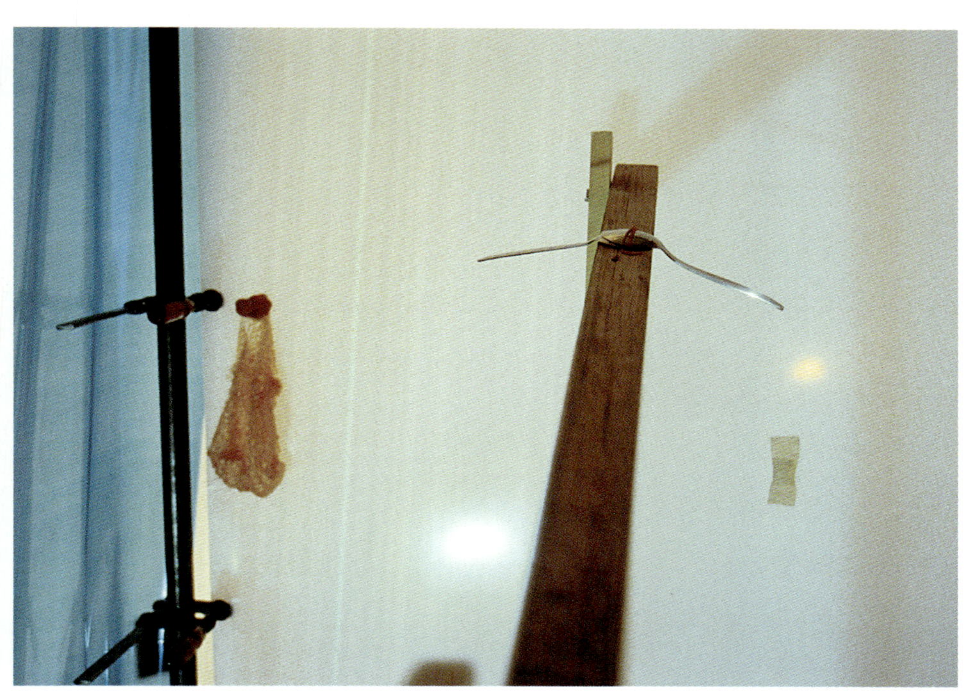

Die Tapferkeit oder das Stärkersein als man selbst (Große Projektion) setzt sich aus zwei Teilen zusammen: einem raumfüllenden, installativen und einem videotechnischen Teil. Teil 1 besteht aus einem nur bedingt einsehbaren Bau aus Folien, weißen Plexiglasscheiben, Holz- und Eisenstangen und einem notdürftig zusammengebauten Verschlag (gerade zu klein für einen Menschen), Neonröhren, Baustellenscheinwerfern, Schneebällen aus Styropor, Glasplatten, Fädchen mit Knoten, Gipsbinden, Hansaplast, Knete und belanglosen Haushaltsgegenständen wie zwei balancierende Löffelchen, Gummibänder, Zitronennetz und Vittelflasche mit einem Rest Mineralwasser. Wie bei einem dreiseitigen Kartenhaus sind die Dinge aneinander gestellt und stabilisieren sich gegenseitig. Anstelle der fehlenden vierten Wand steht ein labiles Holzgestell mit einem Diaprojektor, der sich auf einem elektrischen Drehmotor langsam im Kreis dreht und den gesamten Aufbau wie ein Suchscheinwerfer beleuchtet. Der kleine Verschlag verbirgt seinen Inhalt weitgehend vor dem Auge des Betrachters. Teil 2 vervollständigt die ›Große Projektion‹: Auf einem Monitor wird eine Kamerafahrt durch Teil 1 und den Inhalt des kleinen Verschlags gezeigt. Man sieht eine Wolldecke, eine flackernde Glühbirne, eine kleine, leere Glasvitrine und eine Schwarzweißfotografie derselben. Außerdem gehört zum Teil 2 eine zwei mal zwei Meter große Videoprojektion, die eine Außenwand von Teil 1 zeigt: die halbtransparente Plexiglasscheibe mit dem vom rotierenden Diaprojektor und anderen Lichtquellen erzeugten, wandernden Schattenbild. *Braveness or Being Stronger than Oneself (Large Projection) is composed of two parts: a room-filling, installative element and a video part. Part 1 features a small structure – its inside only partially discernible – made from foil, sheets of white Plexiglas, wood and iron bars, a makeshift shack (just a little too small for a person), neon lights, floodlights, snowballs made from Styrofoam, sheet glass, small knotted threads, plaster bandages, Band-Aid, play dough and banal household items such as two balanced teaspoons, rubber bands, a lemon net and a Vittel bottle containing leftover mineral water. As with a three-walled house of cards, the objects structure depend on each other for stability. The fourth wall is made up of a wobbly wooden rack with a slide projector placed on the slowly turning disk of a rotary motor, illuminating the entire structure like a searchlight. Part 2 is meant to complete ›Large Projection‹: A camera drive through Part 1 and the inside of the small shack are projected onto a screen. The monitor reveals a woolen blanket, a flickering bulb, a small, empty showcase and its corresponding black-and-white photograph. Part 2 also includes a two-by-two-meter video projection showing an outer wall of Part 1: the semi-transparent sheet of Plexiglas with the moving shadowgraphs made by the rotating slide projector and other light sources.*

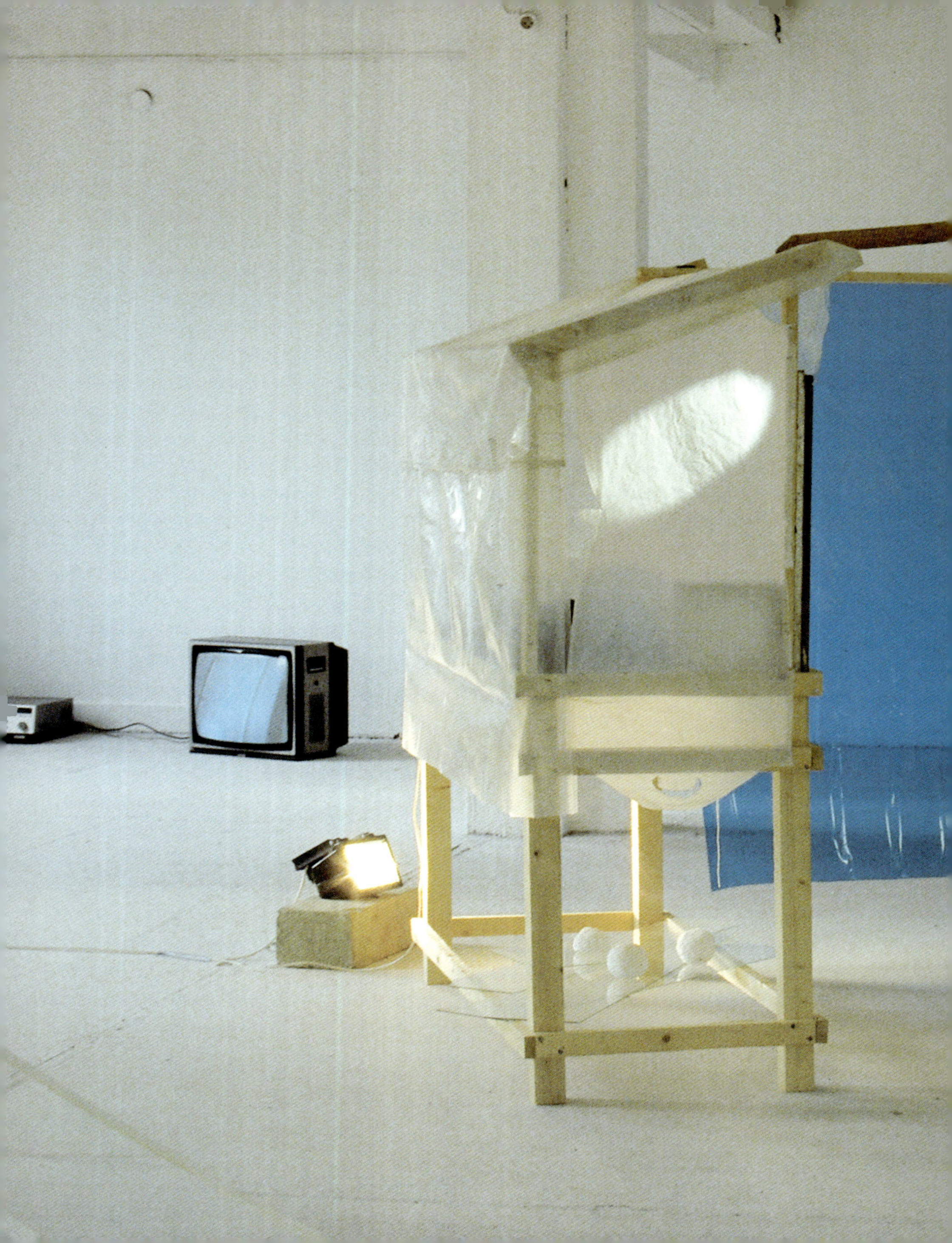

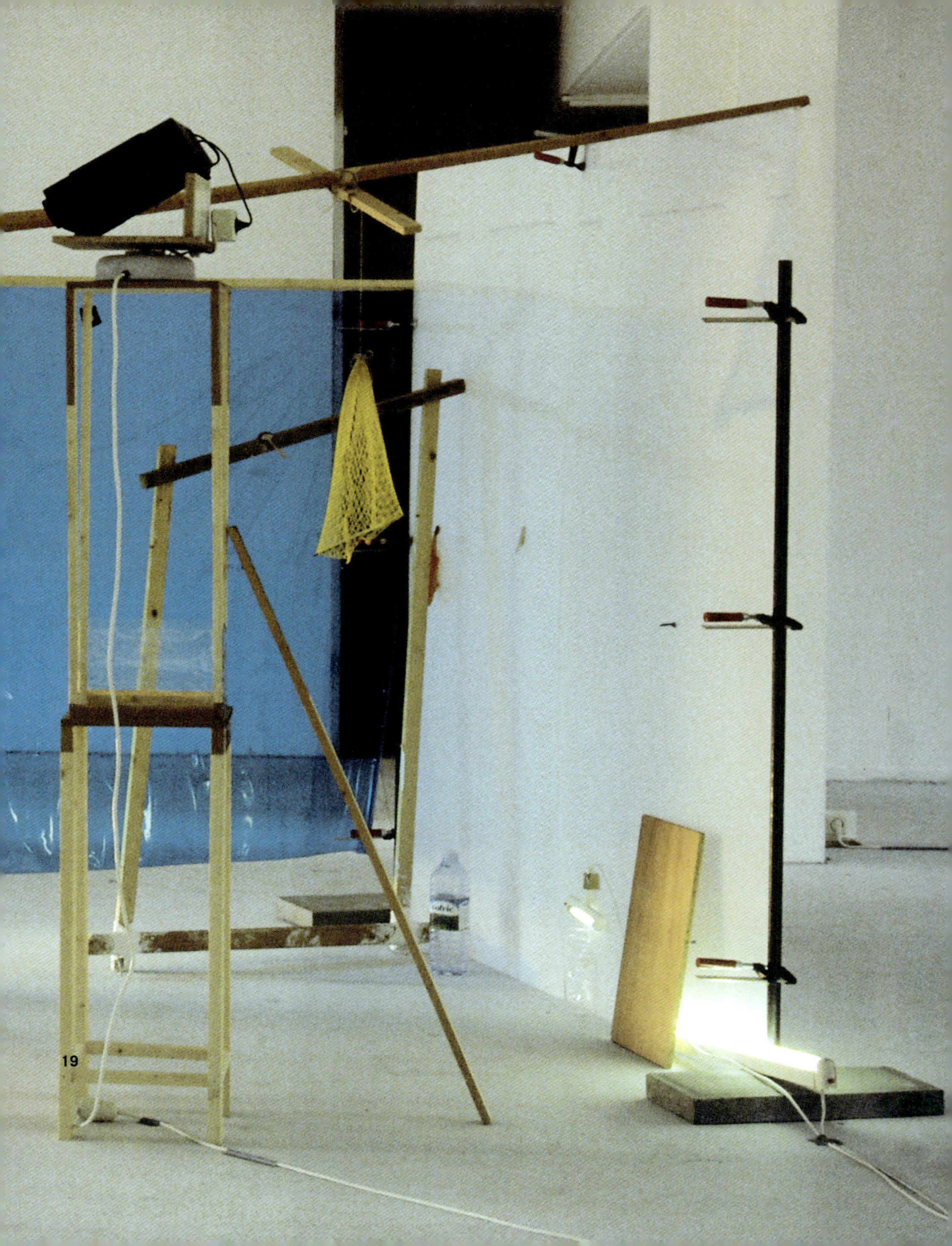

19

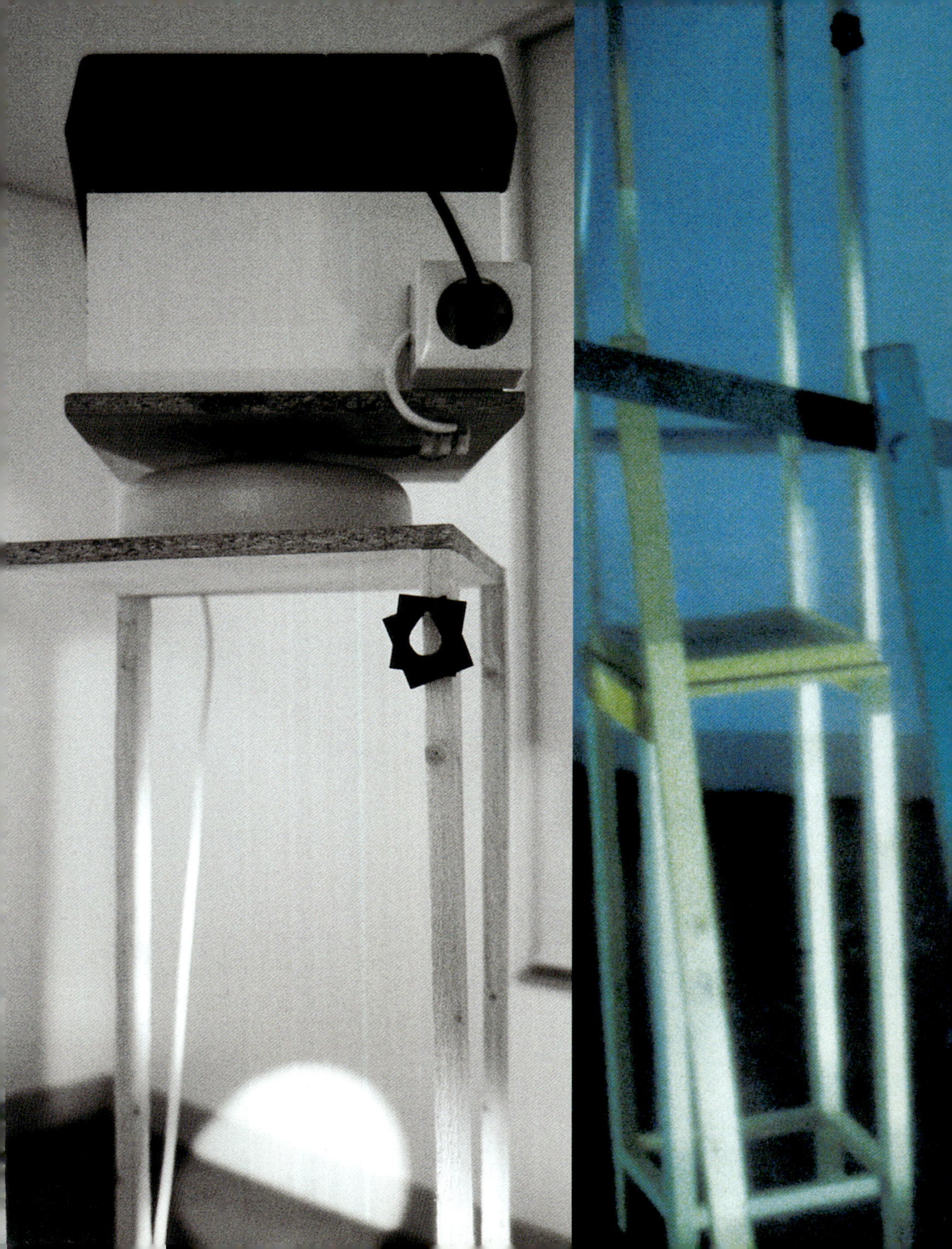

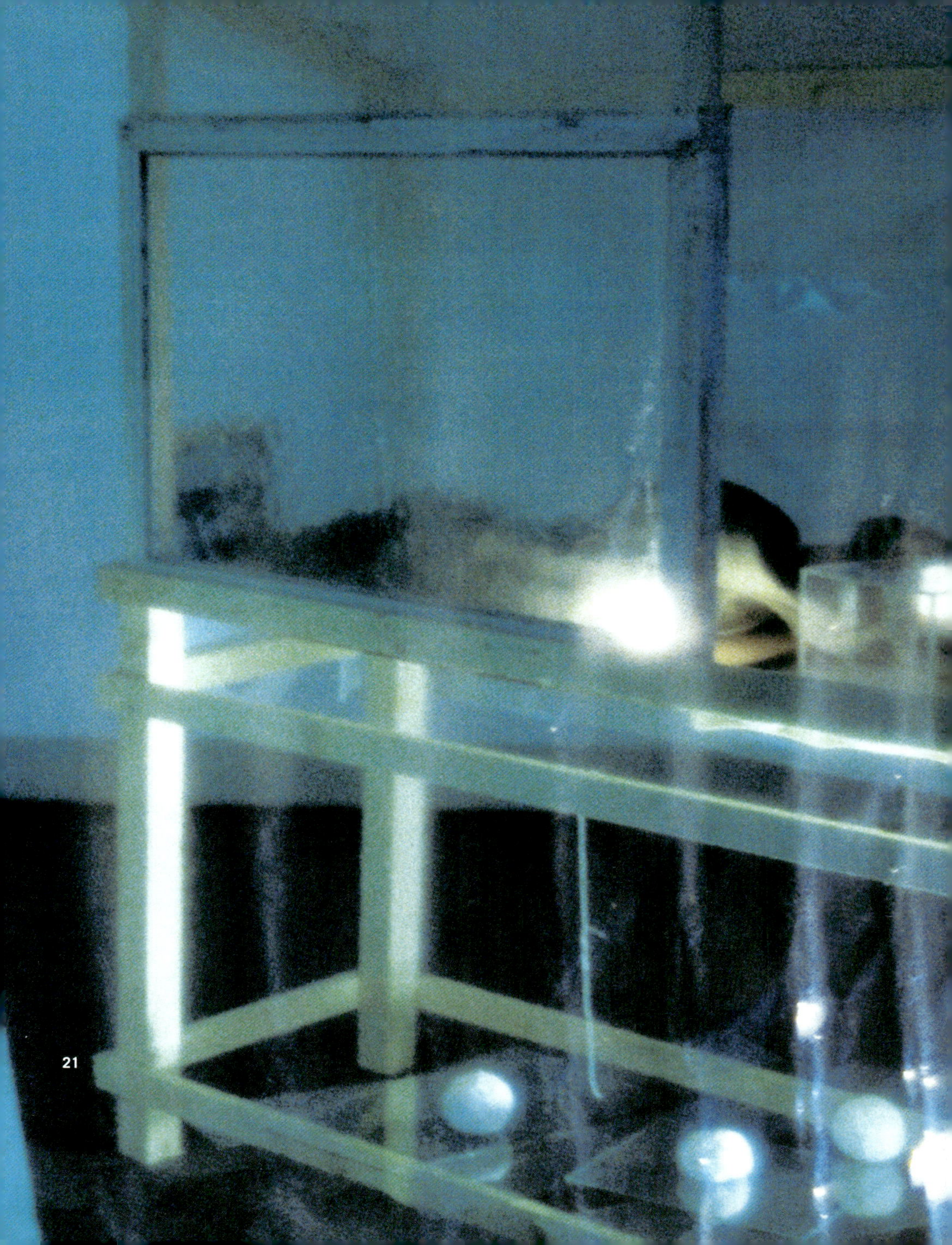

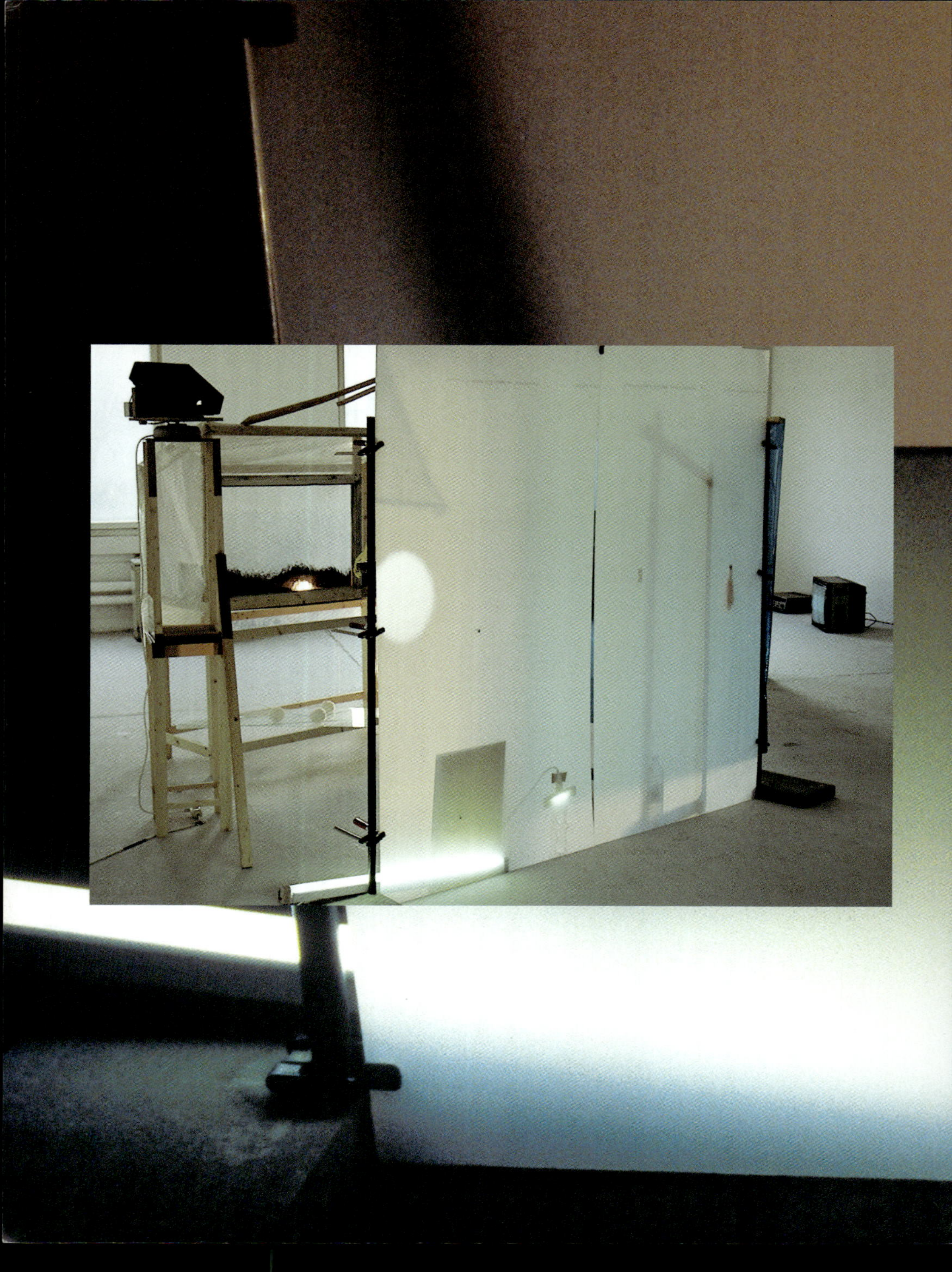

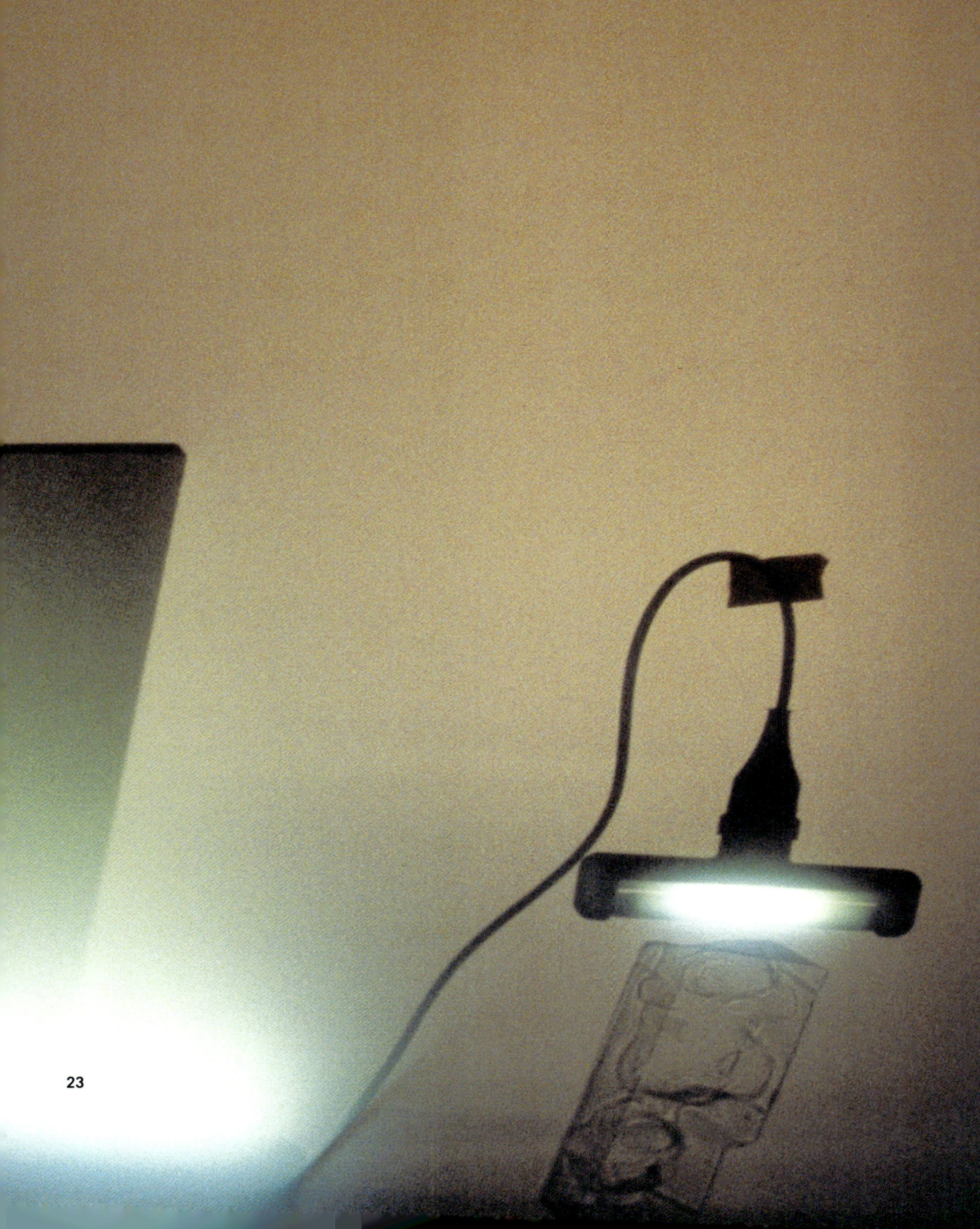

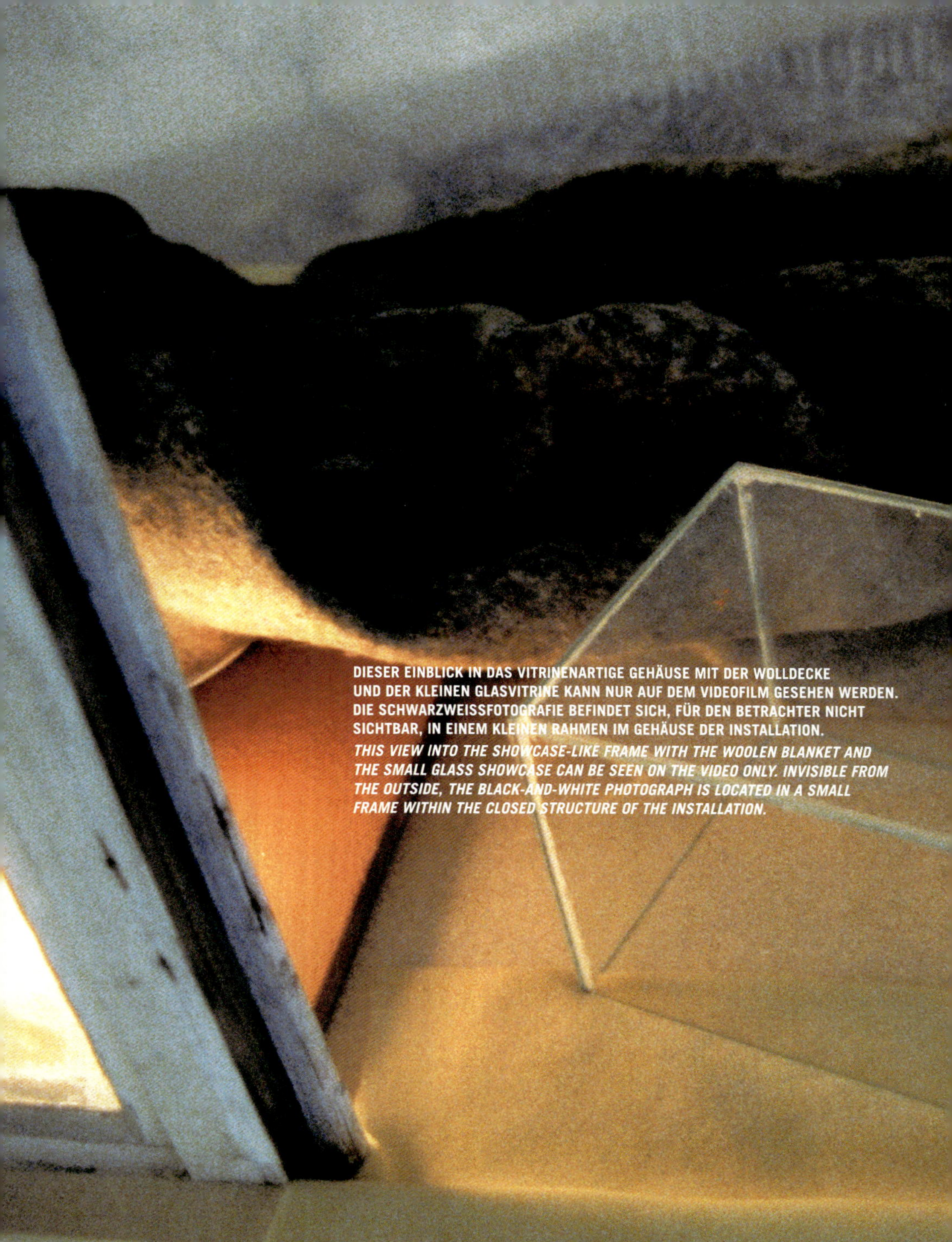

DIESER EINBLICK IN DAS VITRINENARTIGE GEHÄUSE MIT DER WOLLDECKE
UND DER KLEINEN GLASVITRINE KANN NUR AUF DEM VIDEOFILM GESEHEN WERDEN.
DIE SCHWARZWEISSFOTOGRAFIE BEFINDET SICH, FÜR DEN BETRACHTER NICHT
SICHTBAR, IN EINEM KLEINEN RAHMEN IM GEHÄUSE DER INSTALLATION.
*THIS VIEW INTO THE SHOWCASE-LIKE FRAME WITH THE WOOLEN BLANKET AND
THE SMALL GLASS SHOWCASE CAN BE SEEN ON THE VIDEO ONLY. INVISIBLE FROM
THE OUTSIDE, THE BLACK-AND-WHITE PHOTOGRAPH IS LOCATED IN A SMALL
FRAME WITHIN THE CLOSED STRUCTURE OF THE INSTALLATION.*

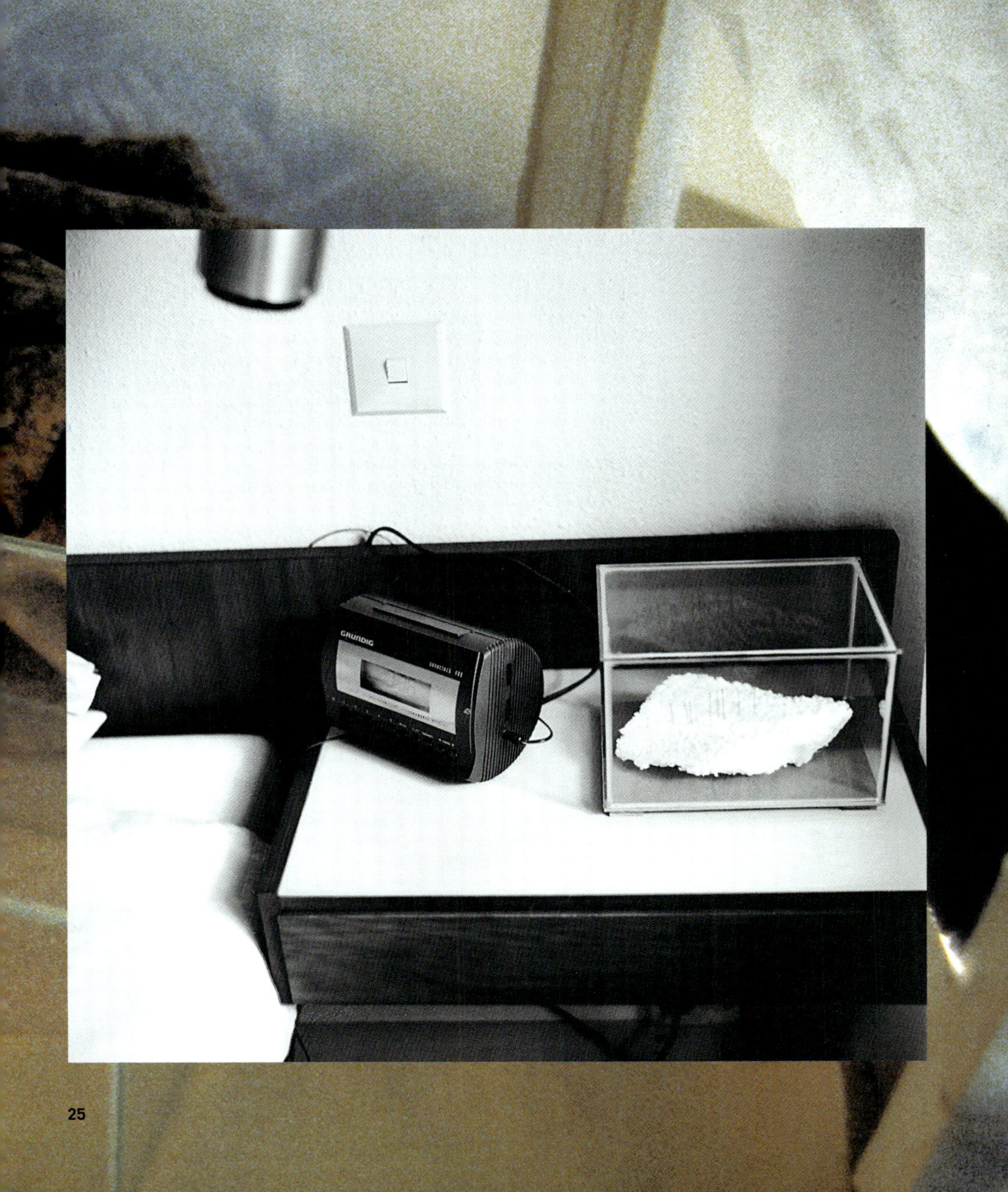

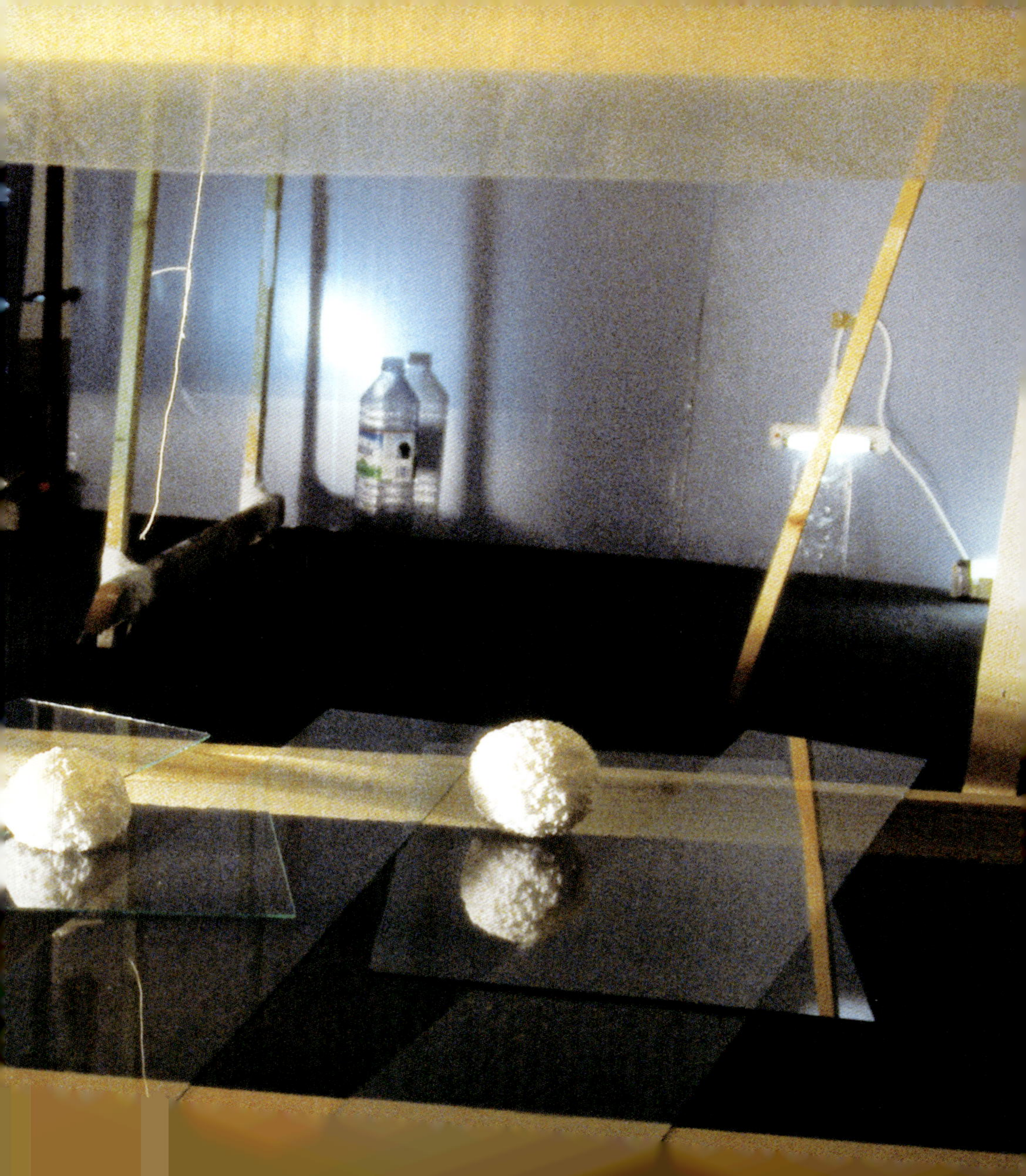

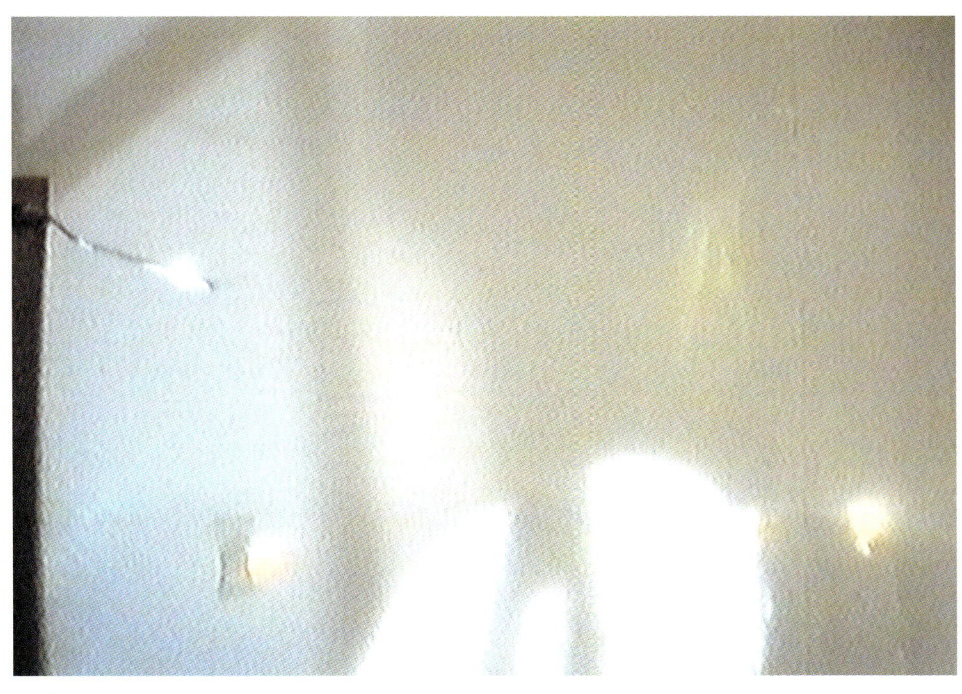

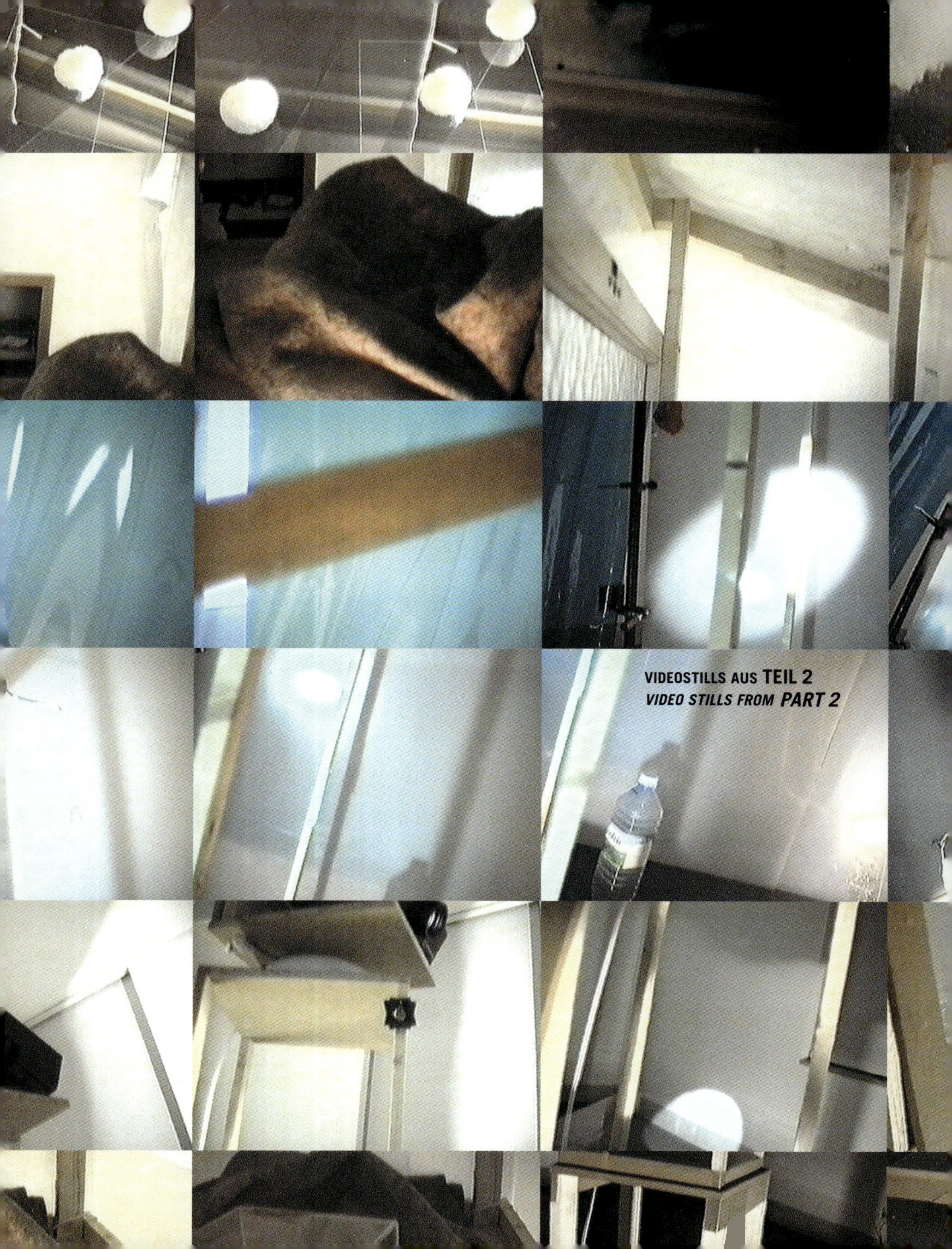
VIDEOSTILLS AUS TEIL 2
VIDEO STILLS FROM PART 2

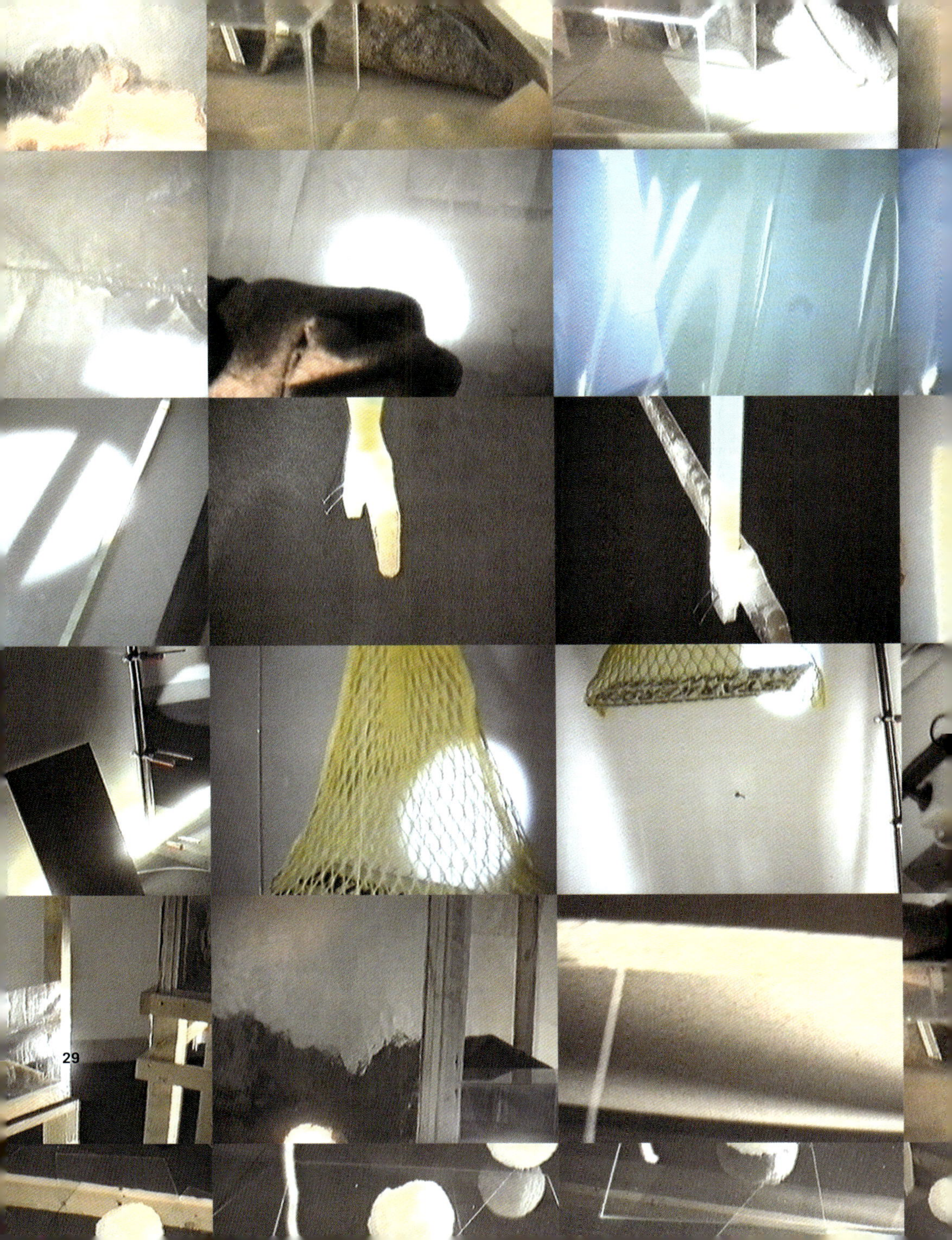

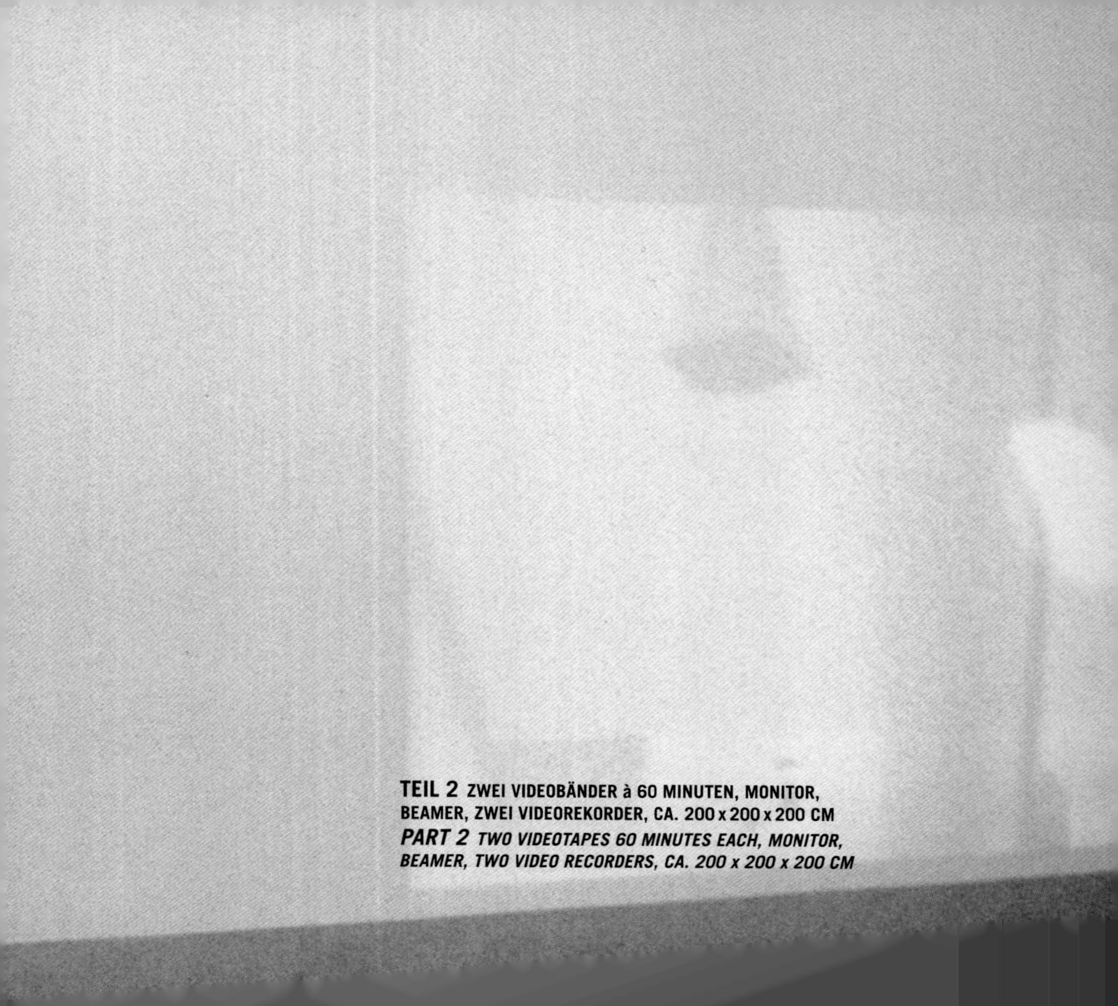

TEIL 2 ZWEI VIDEOBÄNDER à 60 MINUTEN, MONITOR,
BEAMER, ZWEI VIDEOREKORDER, CA. 200 x 200 x 200 CM
PART 2 TWO VIDEOTAPES 60 MINUTES EACH, MONITOR,
BEAMER, TWO VIDEO RECORDERS, CA. 200 x 200 x 200 CM

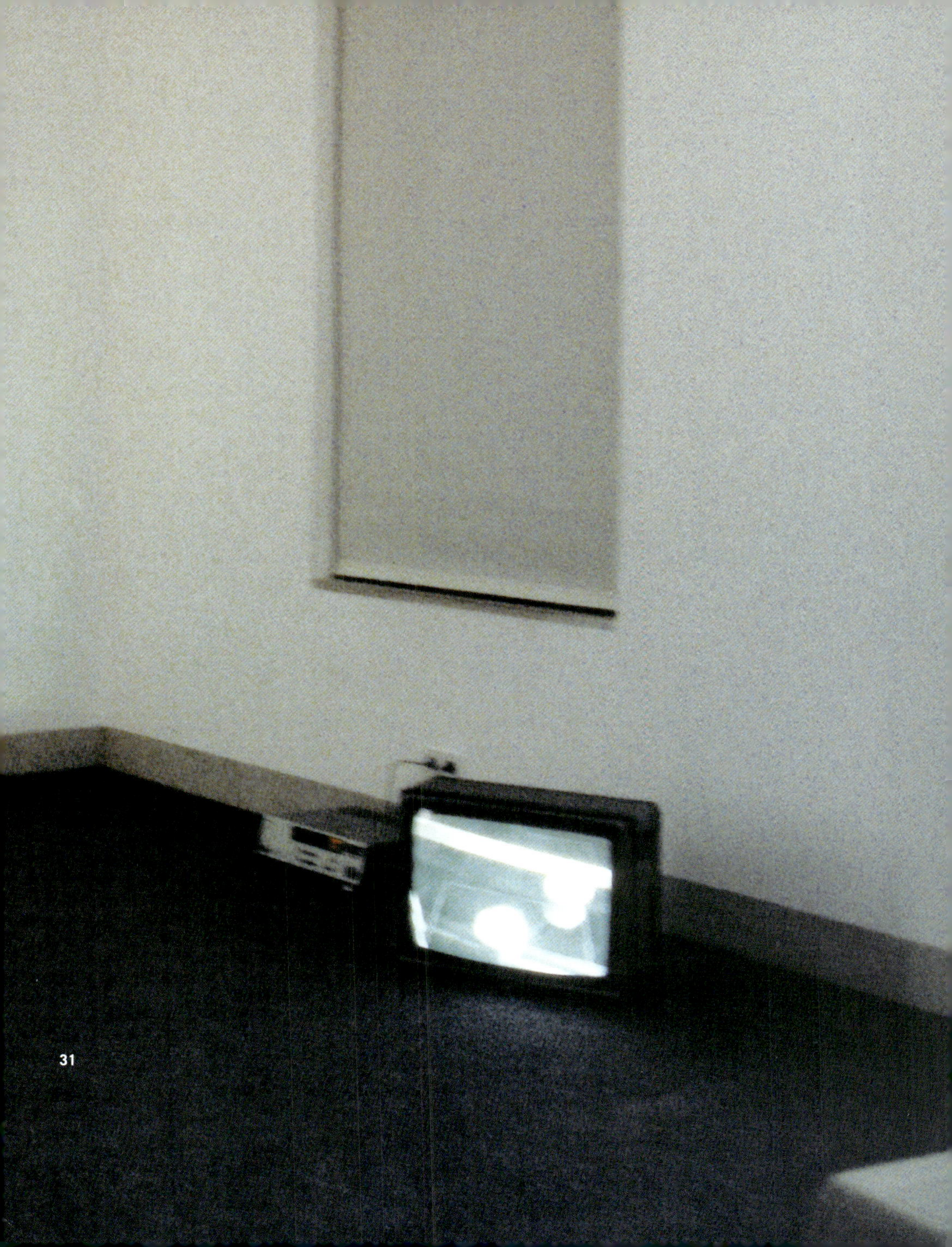

CHRISTOPH TANNERT #1 DEM ›NOCH-NICHT-DETERMINIERTEN‹ AUF DER SPUR Es geht ein Ruck durch Deutschland. Die Verhinderer der Einheit haben ihren ersten Sieg errungen. Die Ästhetik der unaufgeräumten Kinderzimmer bricht sich Bahn, die Verwüstungen nehmen zu, Zusammengehöriges wird auseinander genommen und scheinbar wahllos verteilt. Räume, auch Räume für die Kunst, verlieren ihre zentralen Ideen. Ein neuer Wettstreit um verschiedene ›Mitten‹ entwickelt sich. Kunstwerke mäandern durch den Raum, so als seien sie freigesprochen worden von jeglichen Fokussierungsprozessen. Alles hat mit allem zu tun, nichts ist stärker als der Zusammenschnitt, die Mannigfaltigkeiten triumphieren über das Hierarchische, Sampling allerorten. Wenn Beuys in Deutschland überhaupt geistige Nachfahren haben sollte, dann wollen die möglichst oft und möglichst weit weg von dessen Heil versprechendem Pathos, von Fett und Filz und persuasiver Beredsamkeit. Unbändiger Ausbreitungs- und Bewegungsdrang hat die Sinnsuche abgelöst. Ein sinnvolles Leben ist heute nur mehr ein fremde Territorien besetzendes, bewegtes Leben. Man macht sich einen Spaß daraus, die Grenzwächter von Kunstgeschichte, Musik und Philosophie zu narren. Der Übergriff ist die beste Methode der Verteidigung. Militärexperten werden das bestätigen. Natürlich entscheidet sich am einzelnen Werk selbst, ob das Prinzip der Enthierarchisierung auch eine Verdichtung von Ereignissen provoziert oder sich lediglich in Hilflosigkeit verzettelt. Auf jeden Fall hat die Vorstellung letztgültiger Regelungen ausgedient, was aber nicht heißt, dass ›Maßgelungenheit‹ aus der Mode gekommen sei. ***CHRISTOPH TANNERT #1** TRACKING DOWN THE ›NOT-YET-DETERMINED‹ Shock waves are running through Germany. The detractors of unity have won their first victory. The aesthetics of chaotic playrooms has taken over, devastations are multiplying, that which belongs together is being taken apart and spread around at random, or so it seems. Spaces, even art spaces, are losing their focus. A new rivalry about respective ›centres‹ is in the making. Works of art are meandering through space as if they were exempt from finding focus altogether. Everything is related to everything, nothing wields more power than the blend, variety triumphs over the hierarchical, sampling is omnipresent. If Beuys has any spiritual successors in Germany at all, they usually aim at the greatest distance from his pathos of salvation, from fat and felt and persuasive eloquence. An untrammelled urge to spread out and move around is replacing the search for meaning. Today, a meaningful life simply is a fast-moving life occupying alien territories. Trying to fool the border guards of art history, music and philosophy has become a common sport. Incursion is the* *best means of defense, as military experts will be glad to confirm. Yet, each work ultimately stands alone in revealing if the principle of de-hierarchization yields a condensation of events, or if a frittering away in helplessness is all that remains. The idea of final rules certainly has had its day, but that does not mean that ›successful balance‹ is out of style, too.*

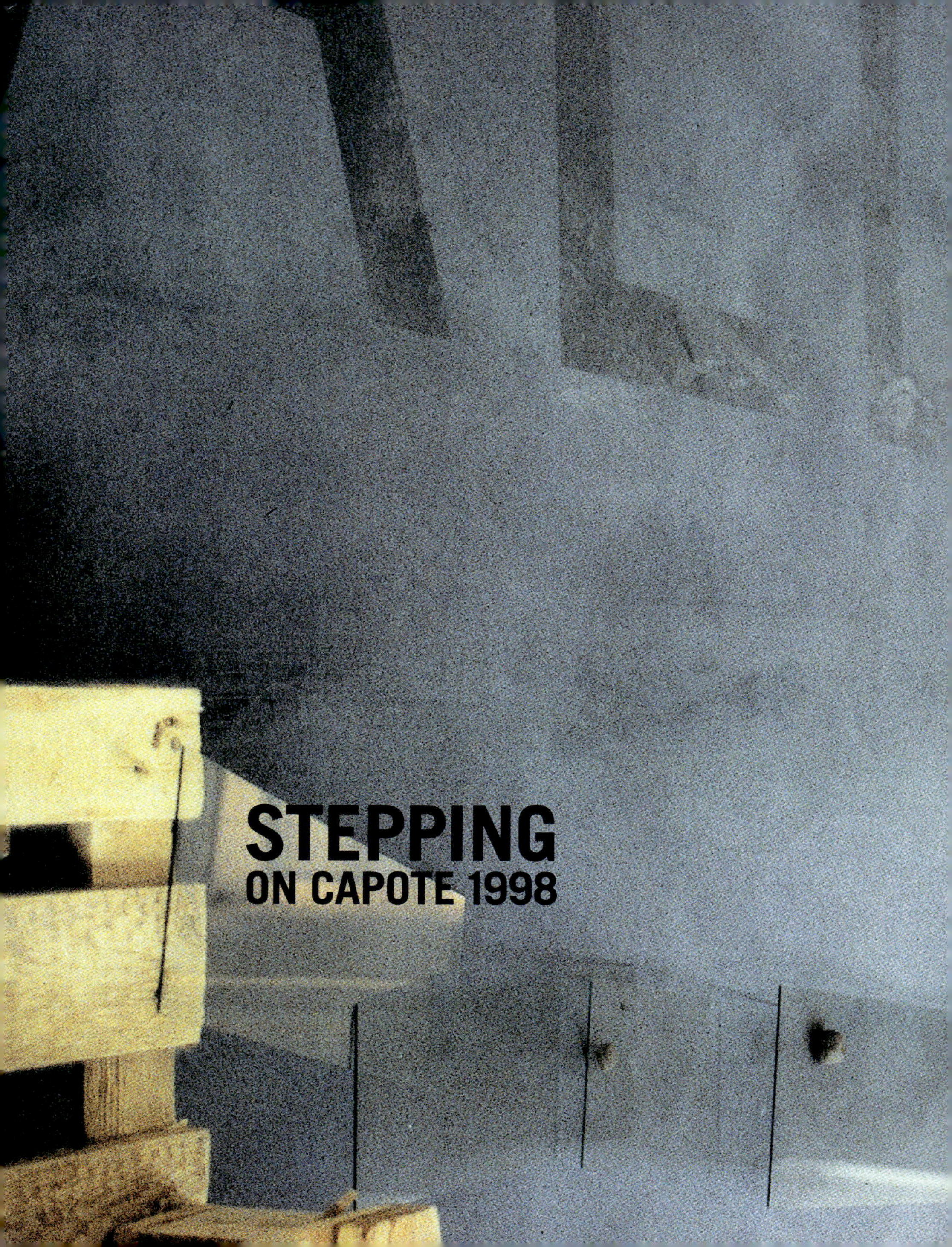
STEPPING
ON CAPOTE 1998

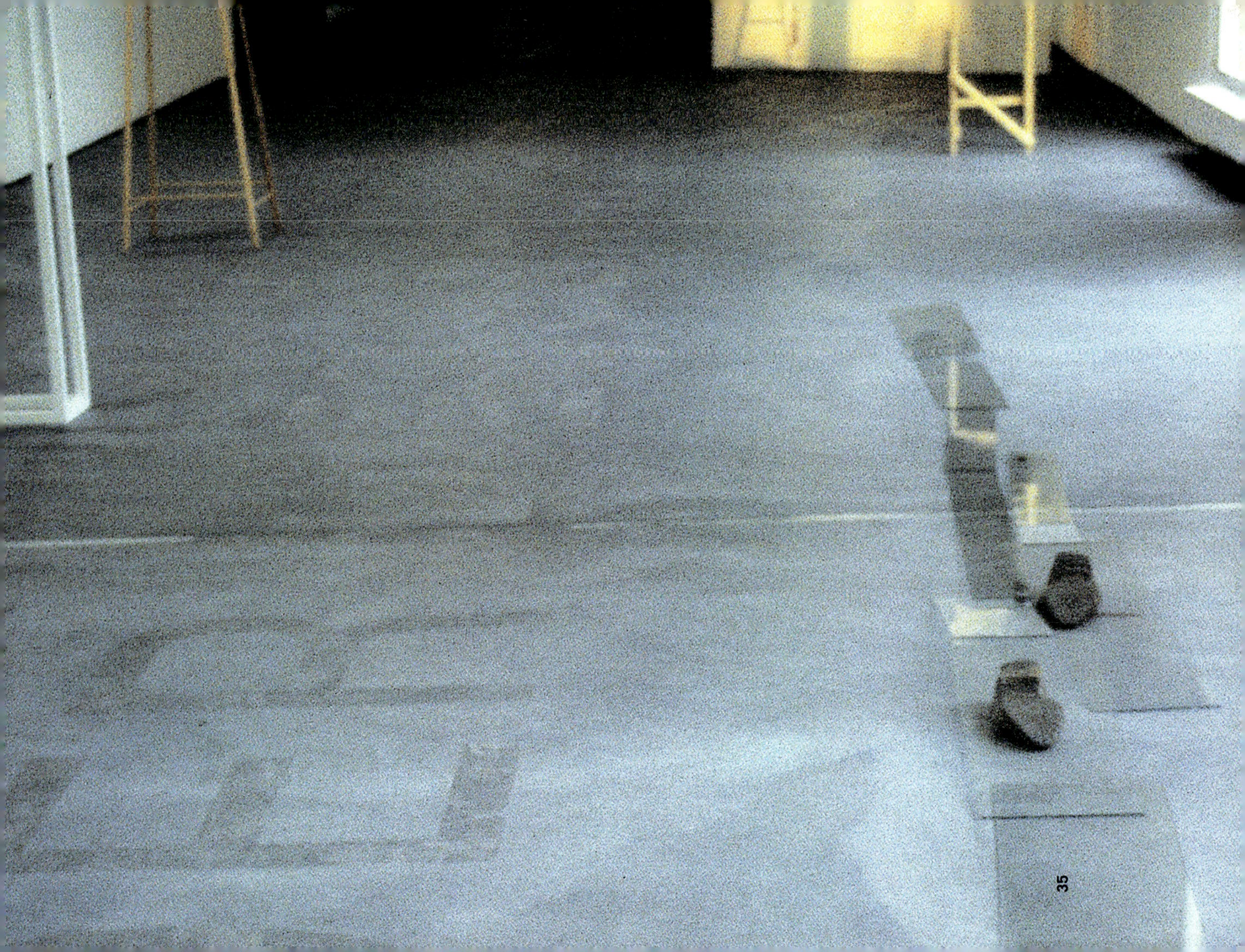

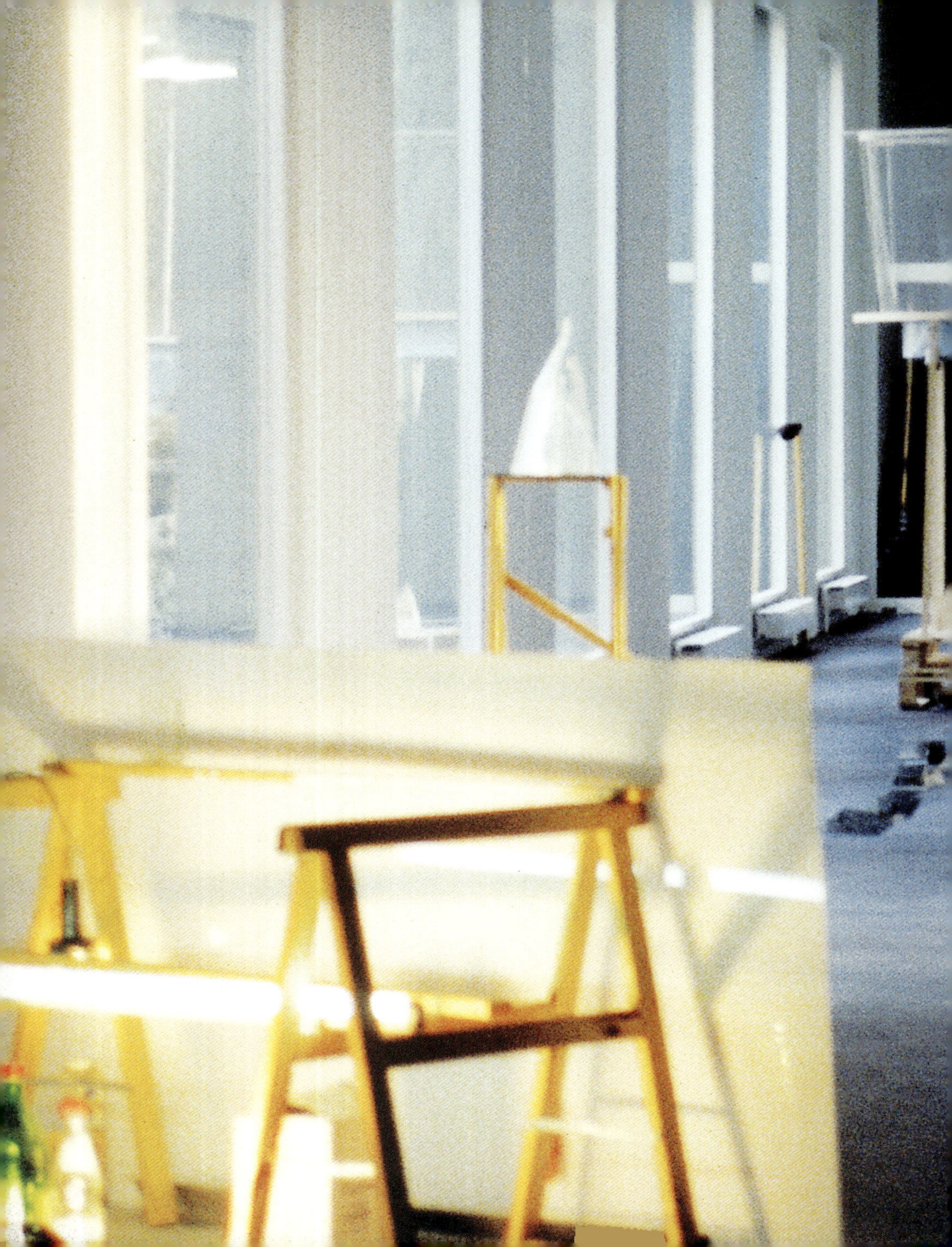

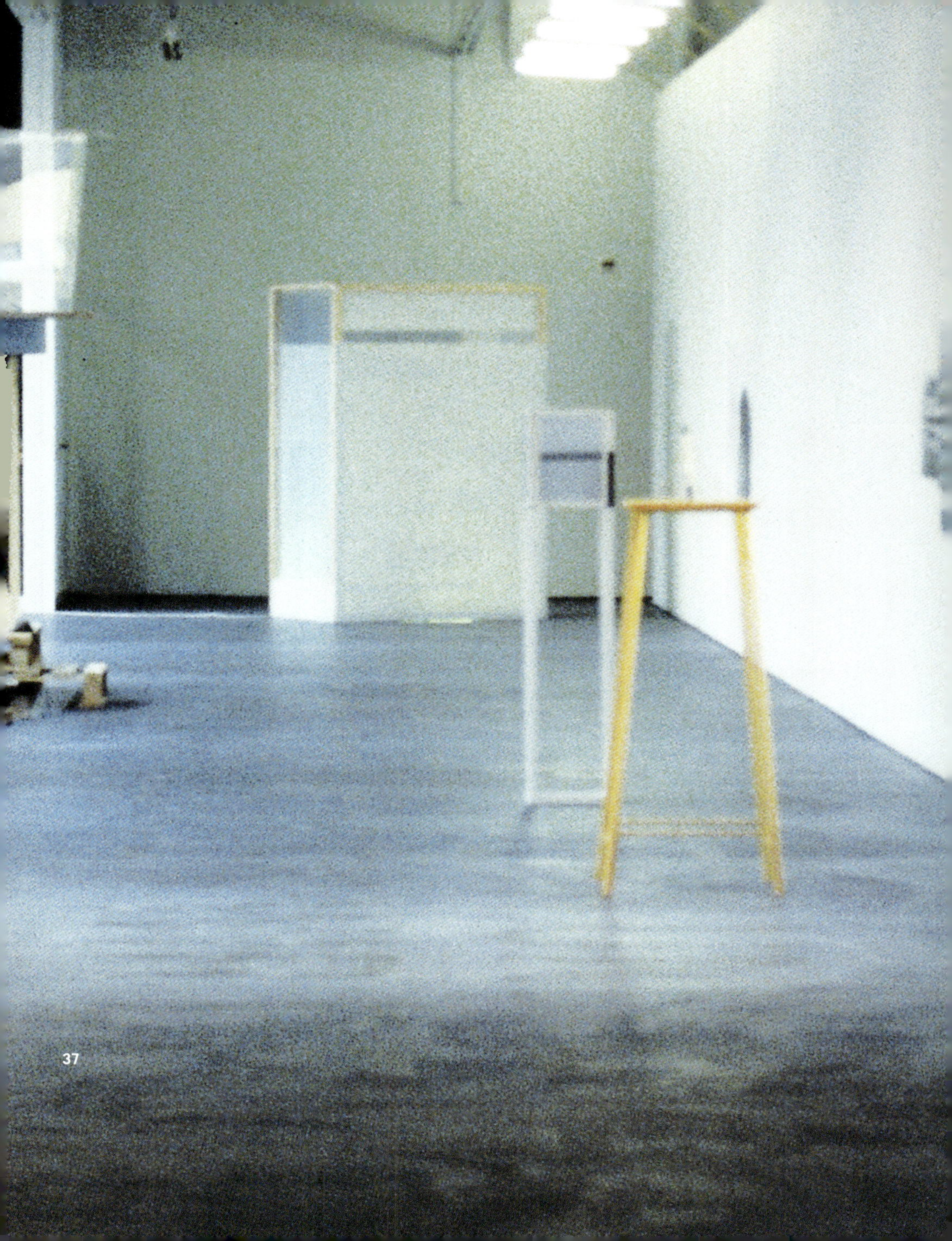

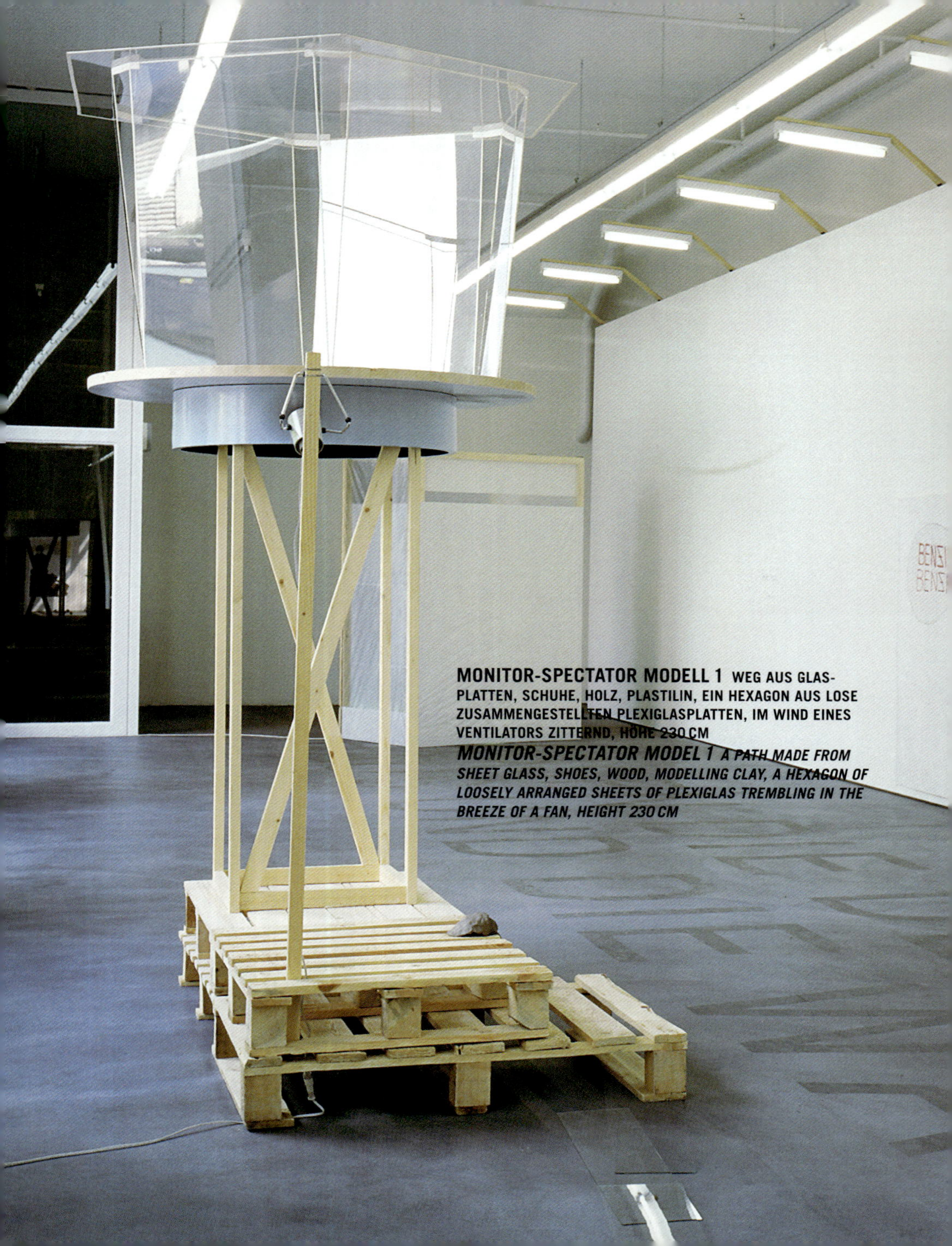

MONITOR-SPECTATOR MODELL 1 WEG AUS GLAS-
PLATTEN, SCHUHE, HOLZ, PLASTILIN, EIN HEXAGON AUS LOSE
ZUSAMMENGESTELLTEN PLEXIGLASPLATTEN, IM WIND EINES
VENTILATORS ZITTERND, HÖHE 230 CM
*MONITOR-SPECTATOR MODEL 1 A PATH MADE FROM
SHEET GLASS, SHOES, WOOD, MODELLING CLAY, A HEXAGON OF
LOOSELY ARRANGED SHEETS OF PLEXIGLAS TREMBLING IN THE
BREEZE OF A FAN, HEIGHT 230 CM*

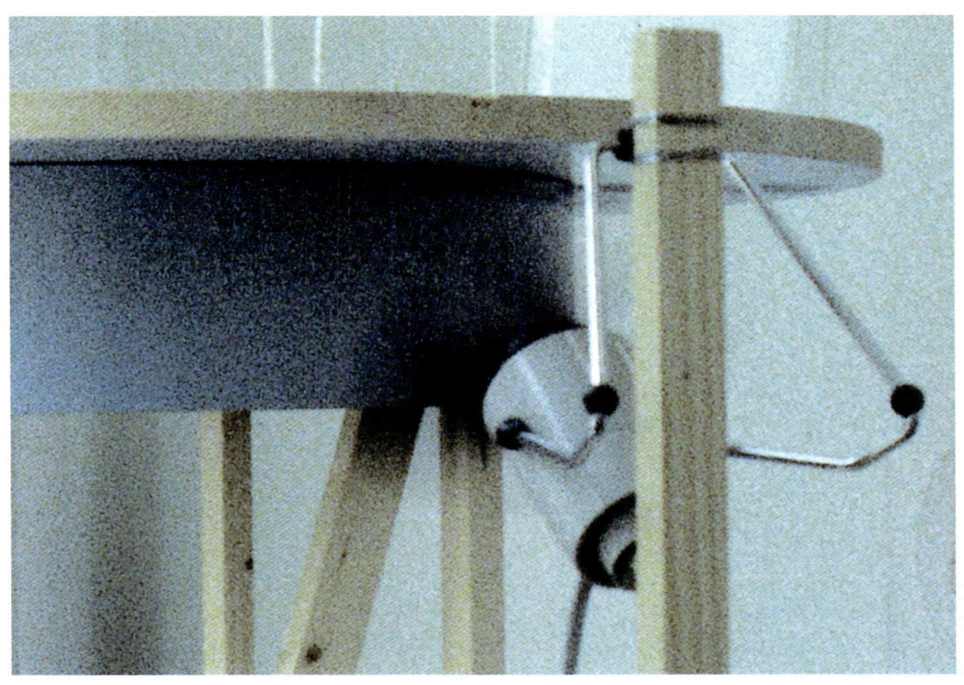

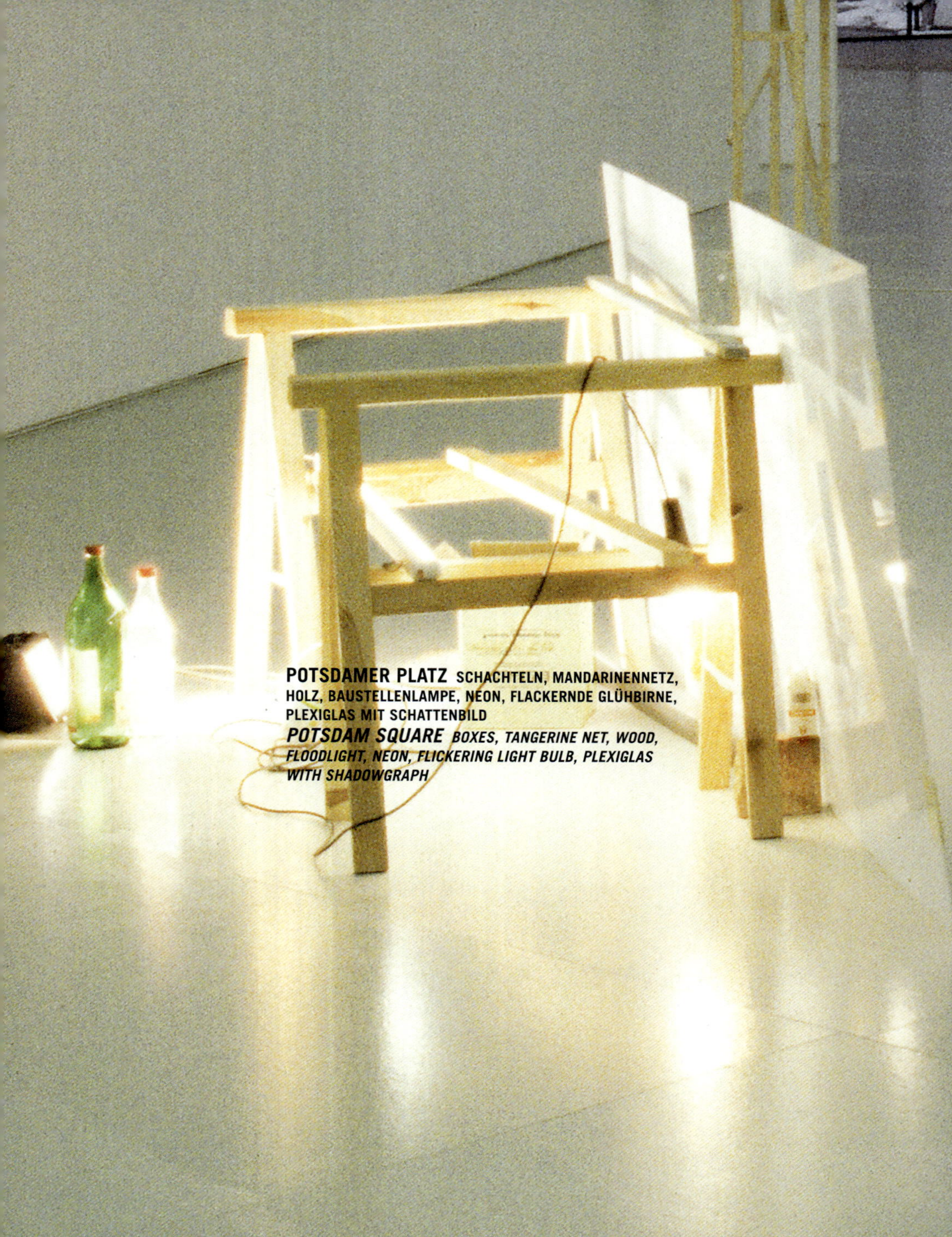

POTSDAMER PLATZ SCHACHTELN, MANDARINENNETZ,
HOLZ, BAUSTELLENLAMPE, NEON, FLACKERNDE GLÜHBIRNE,
PLEXIGLAS MIT SCHATTENBILD
POTSDAM SQUARE BOXES, TANGERINE NET, WOOD,
FLOODLIGHT, NEON, FLICKERING LIGHT BULB, PLEXIGLAS
WITH SHADOWGRAPH

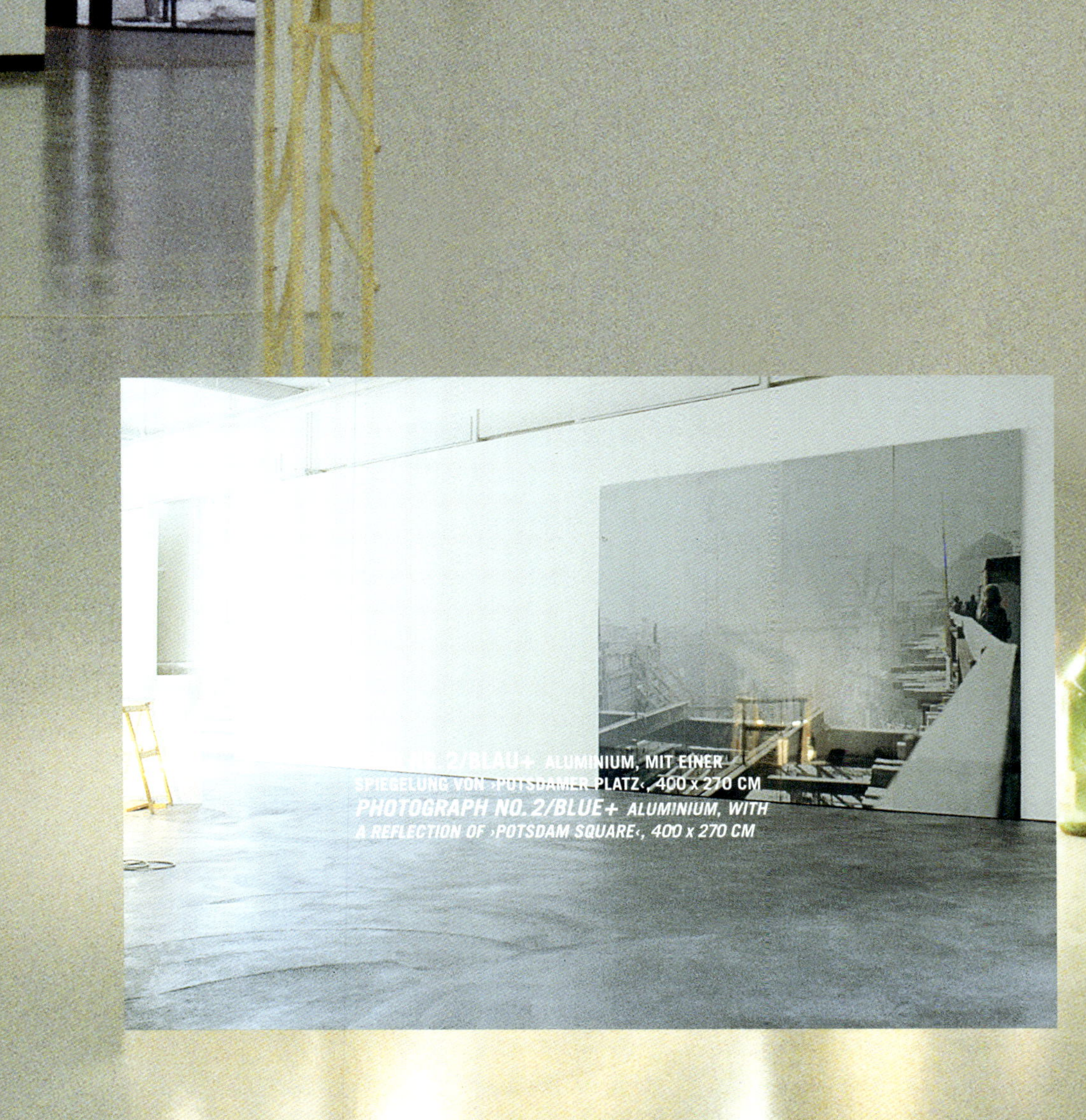
2/BLAU+ ALUMINIUM, MIT EINER
SPIEGELUNG VON ›POTSDAMER PLATZ‹, 400 x 270 CM
PHOTOGRAPH NO. 2/BLUE+ ALUMINIUM, WITH
A REFLECTION OF ›POTSDAM SQUARE‹, 400 x 270 CM

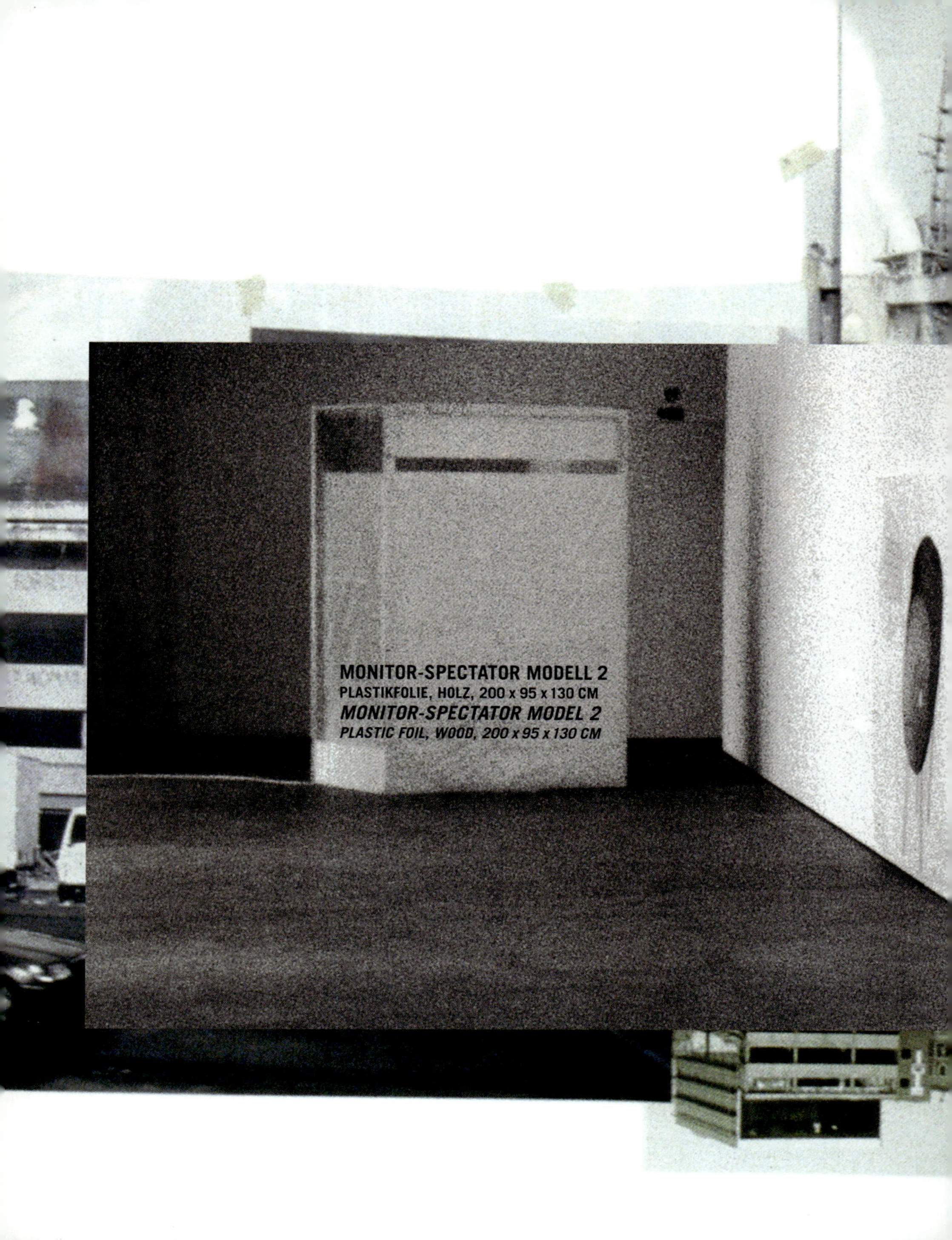
MONITOR-SPECTATOR MODELL 2
PLASTIKFOLIE, HOLZ, 200 x 95 x 130 CM
MONITOR-SPECTATOR MODEL 2
PLASTIC FOIL, WOOD, 200 x 95 x 130 CM

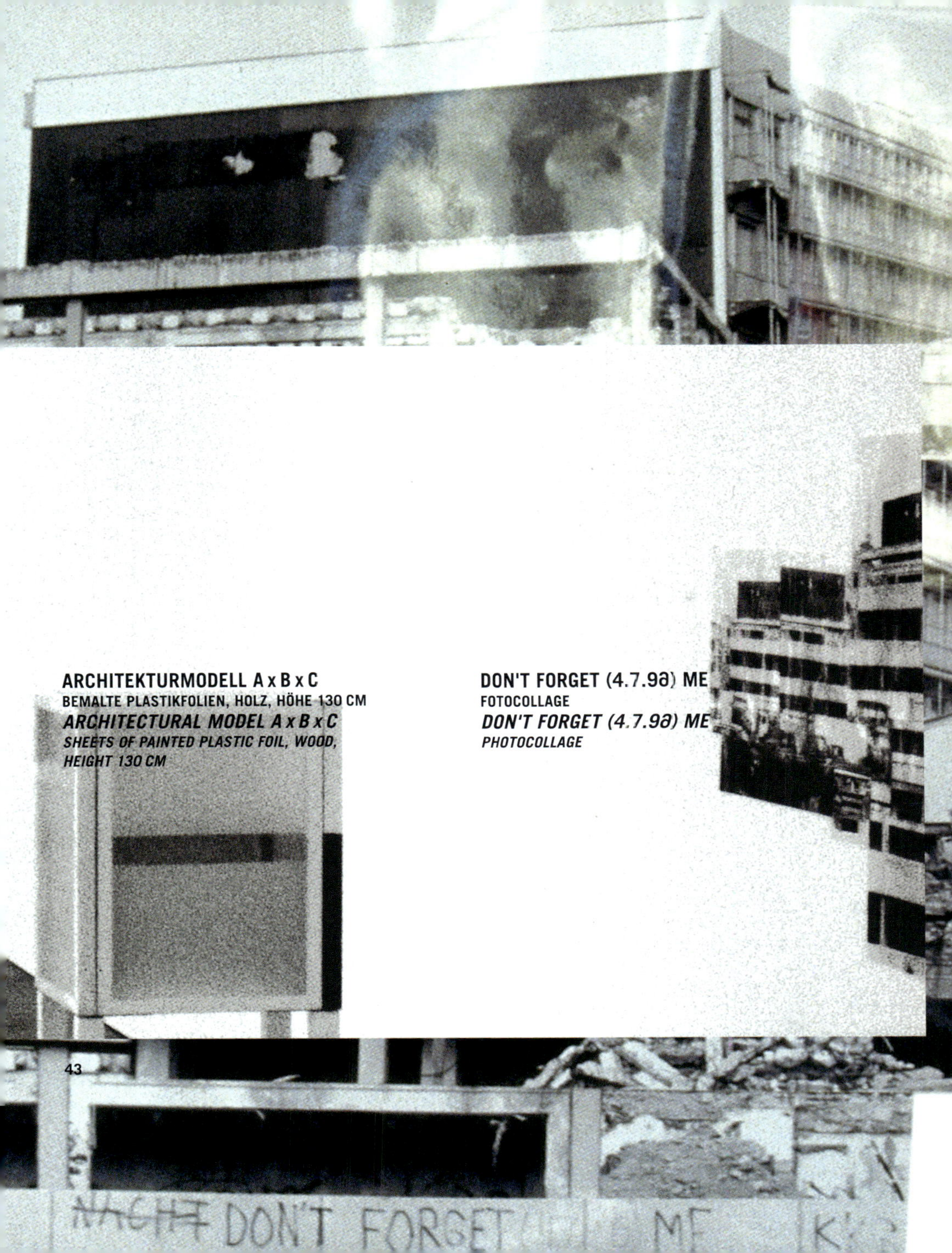

ARCHITEKTURMODELL A x B x C
BEMALTE PLASTIKFOLIEN, HOLZ, HÖHE 130 CM
ARCHITECTURAL MODEL A x B x C
SHEETS OF PAINTED PLASTIC FOIL, WOOD,
HEIGHT 130 CM

DON'T FORGET (4.7.9∂) ME
FOTOCOLLAGE
DON'T FORGET (4.7.9∂) ME
PHOTOCOLLAGE

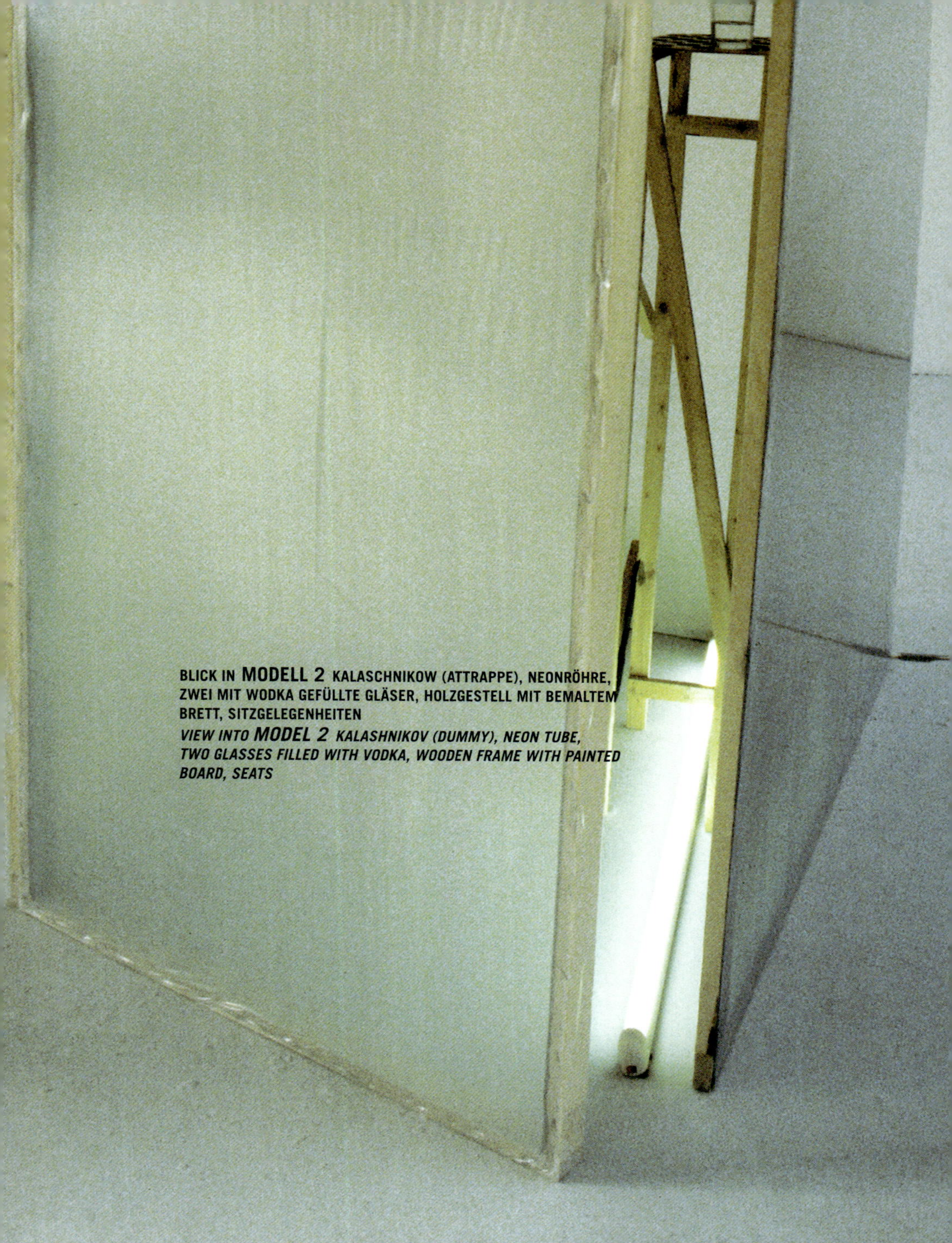

BLICK IN **MODELL 2** KALASCHNIKOW (ATTRAPPE), NEONRÖHRE,
ZWEI MIT WODKA GEFÜLLTE GLÄSER, HOLZGESTELL MIT BEMALTEM
BRETT, SITZGELEGENHEITEN
VIEW INTO **MODEL 2** *KALASHNIKOV (DUMMY), NEON TUBE,
TWO GLASSES FILLED WITH VODKA, WOODEN FRAME WITH PAINTED
BOARD, SEATS*

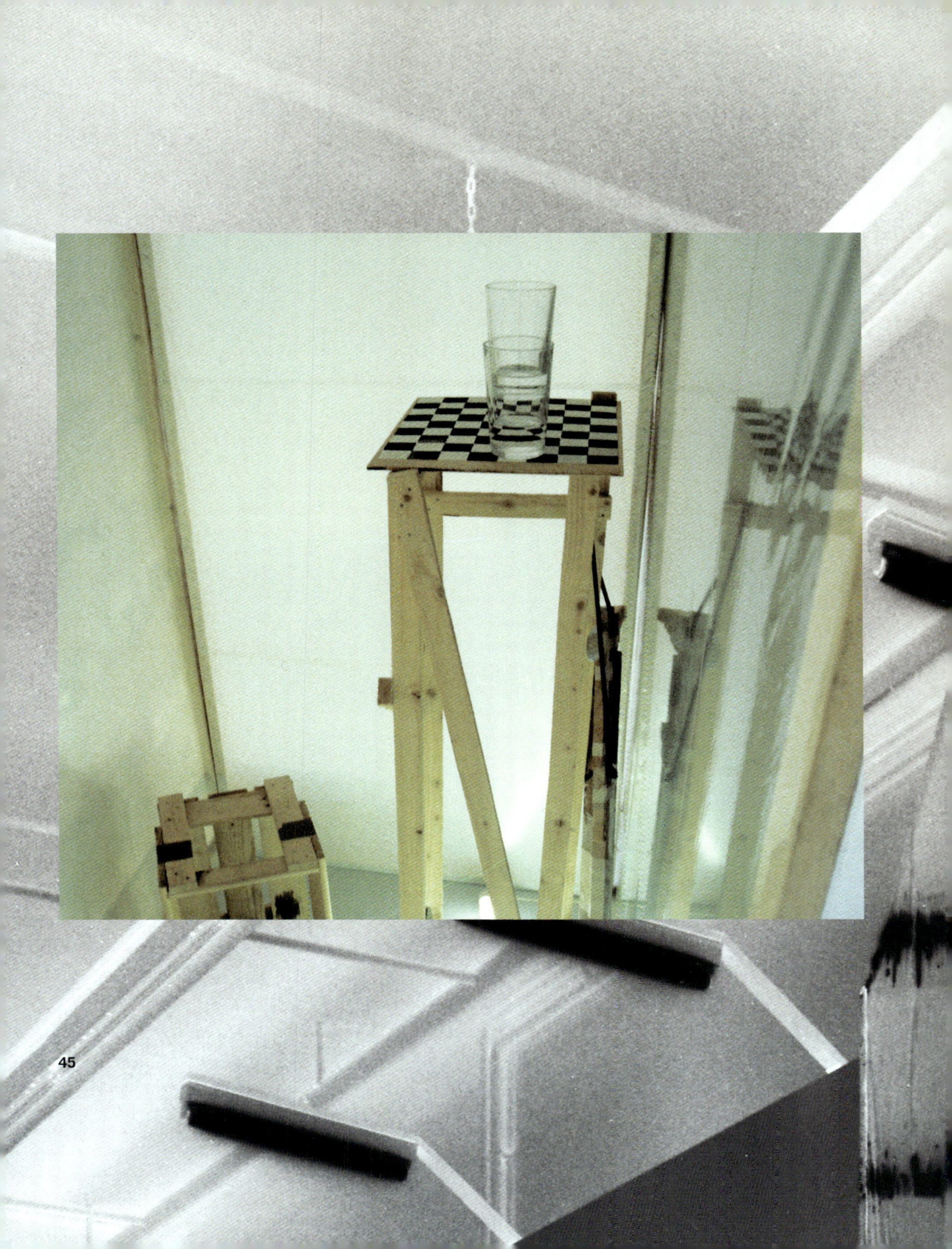

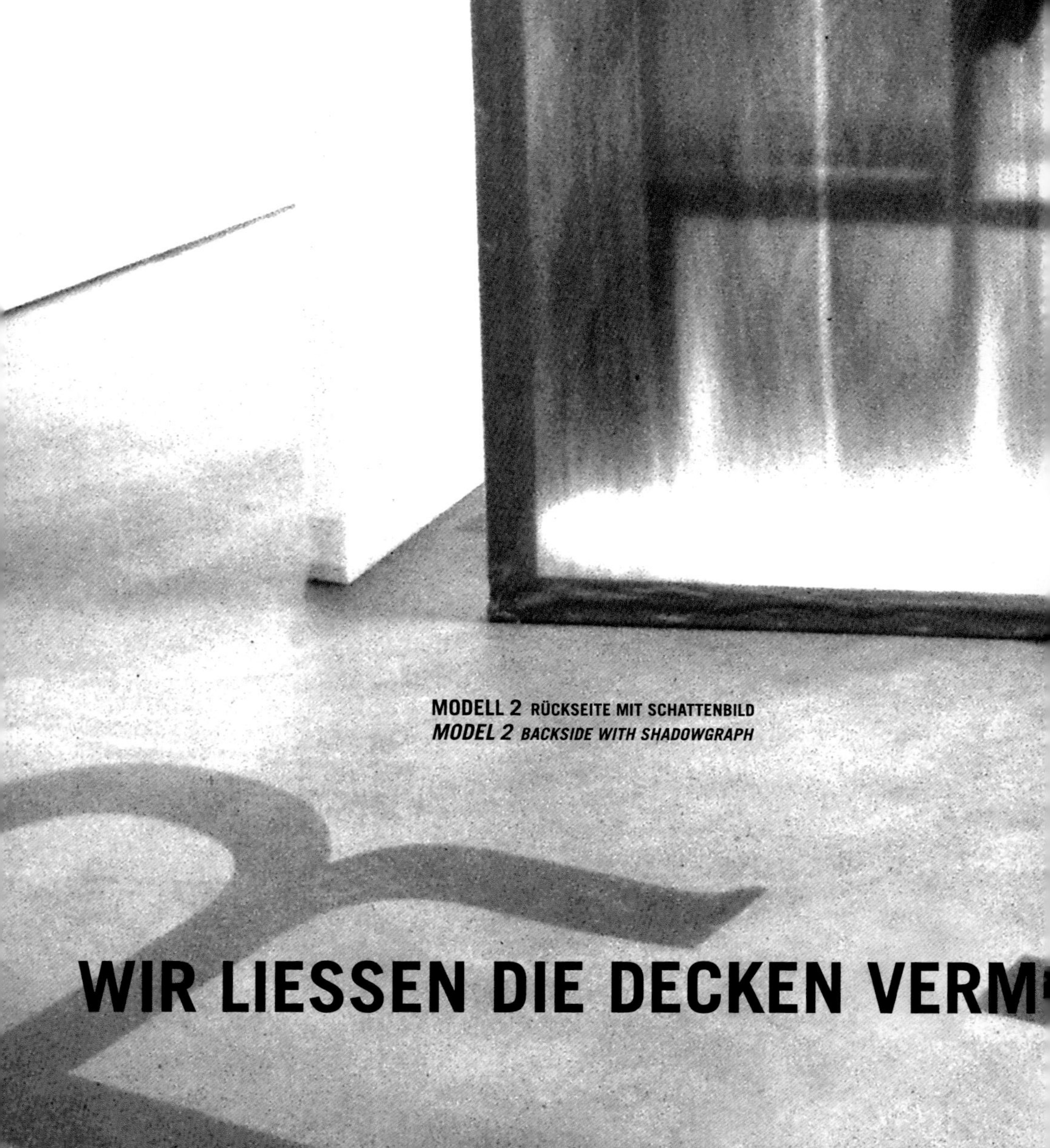

MODELL 2 RÜCKSEITE MIT SCHATTENBILD
MODEL 2 BACKSIDE WITH SHADOWGRAPH

WIR LIESSEN DIE DECKEN VERM

STEPPING ON CAPOTE Die Exponate dieser Rauminstallation (Kunstverein Baselland) sind mehr oder weniger stark ausformulierte Anlehnungen an Bushaltestellen, Baustellen, Unterstände, Wachtürme, Architekturmodelle, Baumhäuser und Benzintanks. Alles fragile Interimslösungen und Zwischenstationen, nicht für einen dauerhaften Aufenthalt bestimmt. Der Betrachter befindet sich auf einer ›Ausstellungsstraße‹, die auch nach oben durch zusätzliche Leuchten definiert wird. Buchstabe für Buchstabe geht man über ein zweizeiliges Zitat von Truman Capote, das die Gesamtsituation räumlich und inhaltlich bündelt. Dabei passiert man Stationen, die allesamt Übergangszustände thematisieren: Momente kurzen Verweilens, für unverhoffte ›prises de conscience‹ anfällige Orte. *STEPPING ON CAPOTE The pieces exhibited in this room installation (Kunstverein Baselland) are phrases of bus stops, construction sites, shelters, watch towers, architectural models, tree houses and gasoline tanks, more or less clearly formulated, all fragile interim solutions and interludes, not meant for permanent residence. Viewers find themselves in an ›exhibition street‹ defined by additional lighting towards the top, tracing, letter by letter, a two-line quotation from Truman Capote which acts as a spatial and textual focus for the situation as a whole while they encounter situations that speak of transitional stages: moments of cursory interest, sites suited to unhoped-for ›prises de conscience‹.*

ERN UND DIE LÖFFEL VERROSTEN,

WE LET THE BLANKETS ROT AND THE SPOONS RUST,

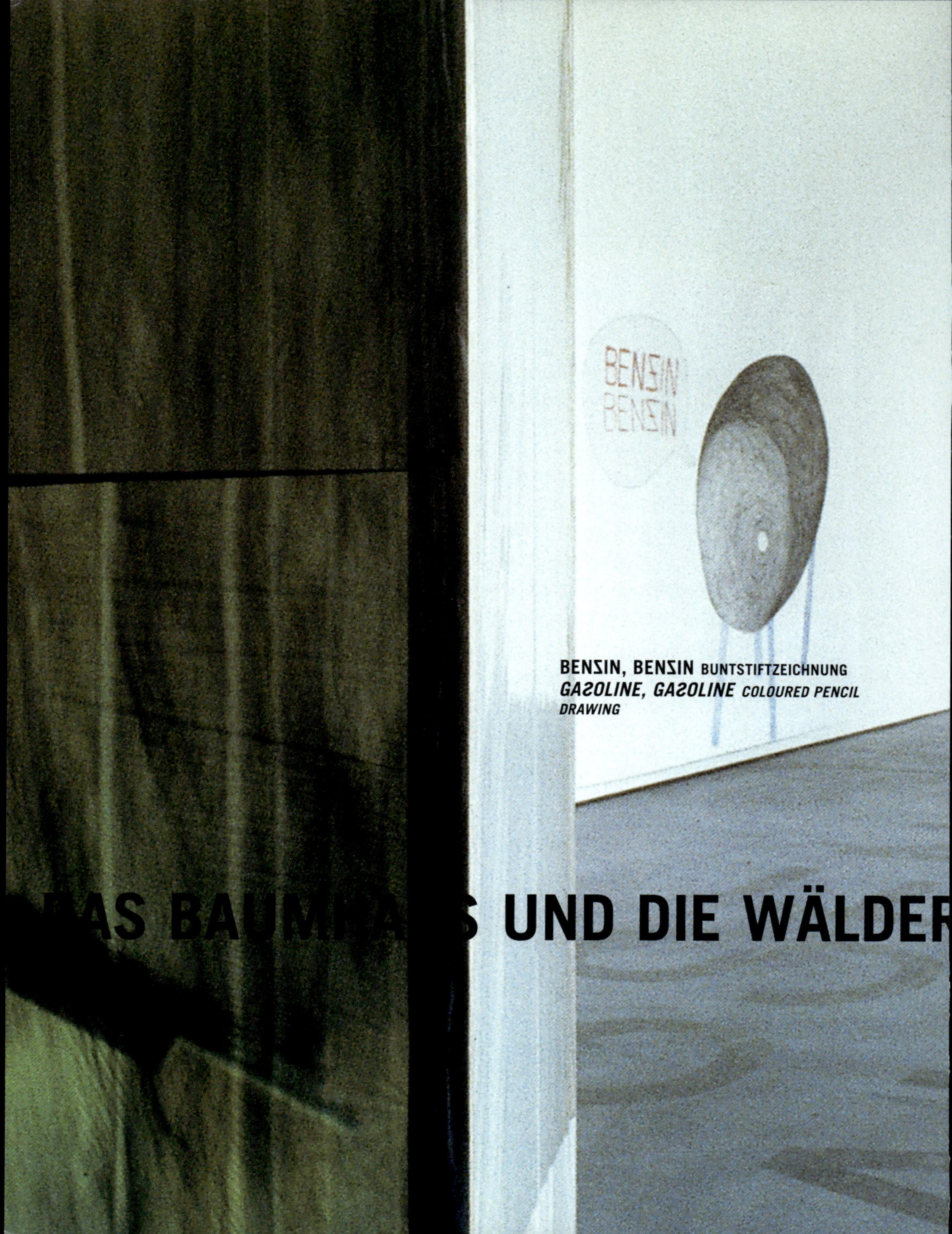

BENSIN
BENSIN
BENSIN, BENSIN BUNTSTIFTZEICHNUNG
GASOLINE, GASOLINE COLOURED PENCIL
DRAWING
AS BAUMHAUS UND DIE WÄLDER

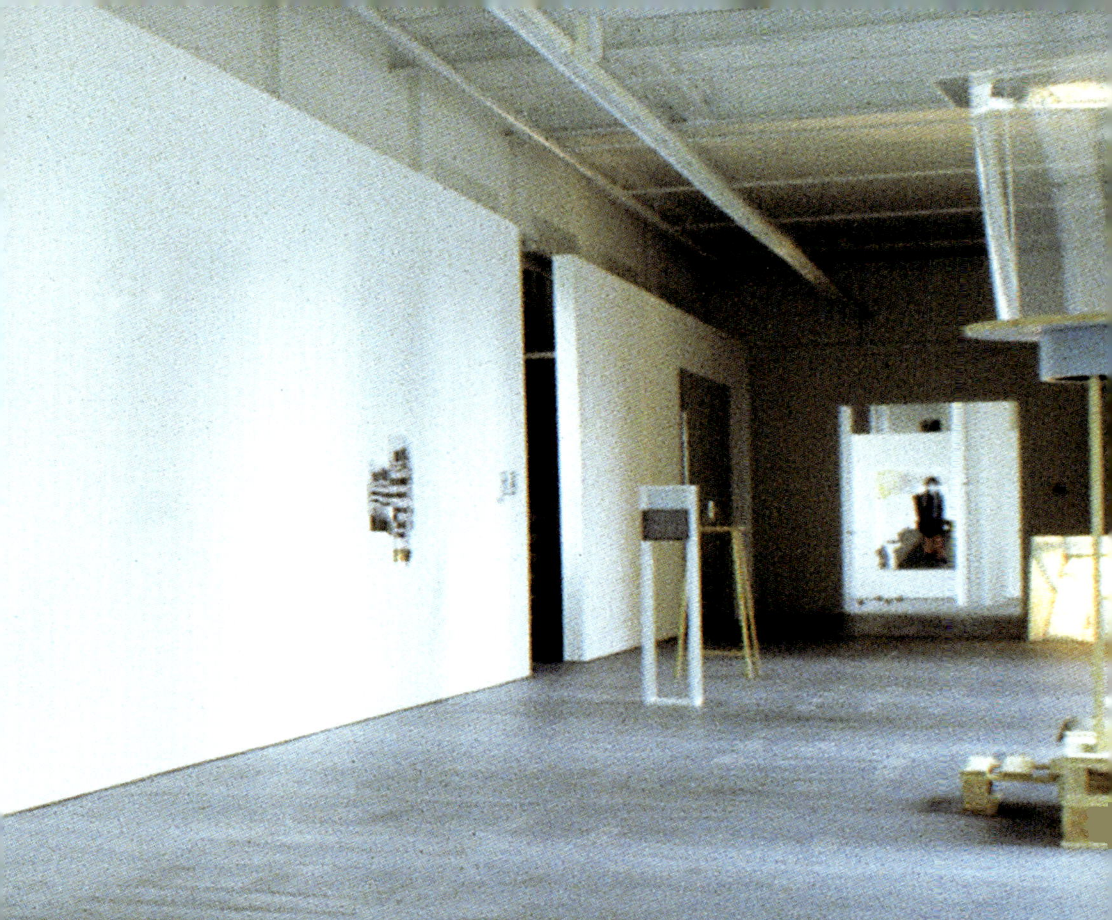

...IESSEN WIR DEM WINTER.
THE TREE HOUSE AND THE WOODS WE LEFT TO THE WINTER.

49

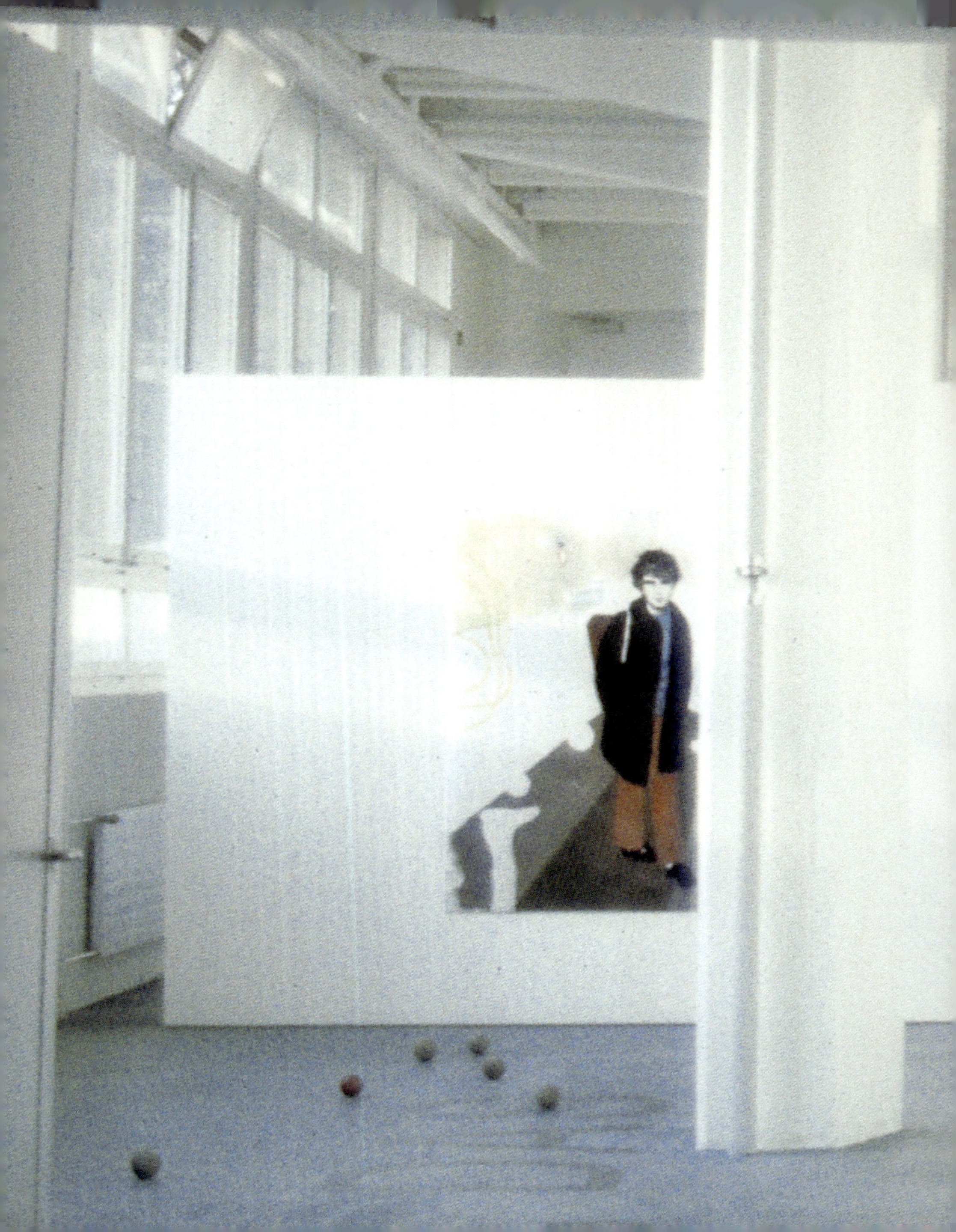

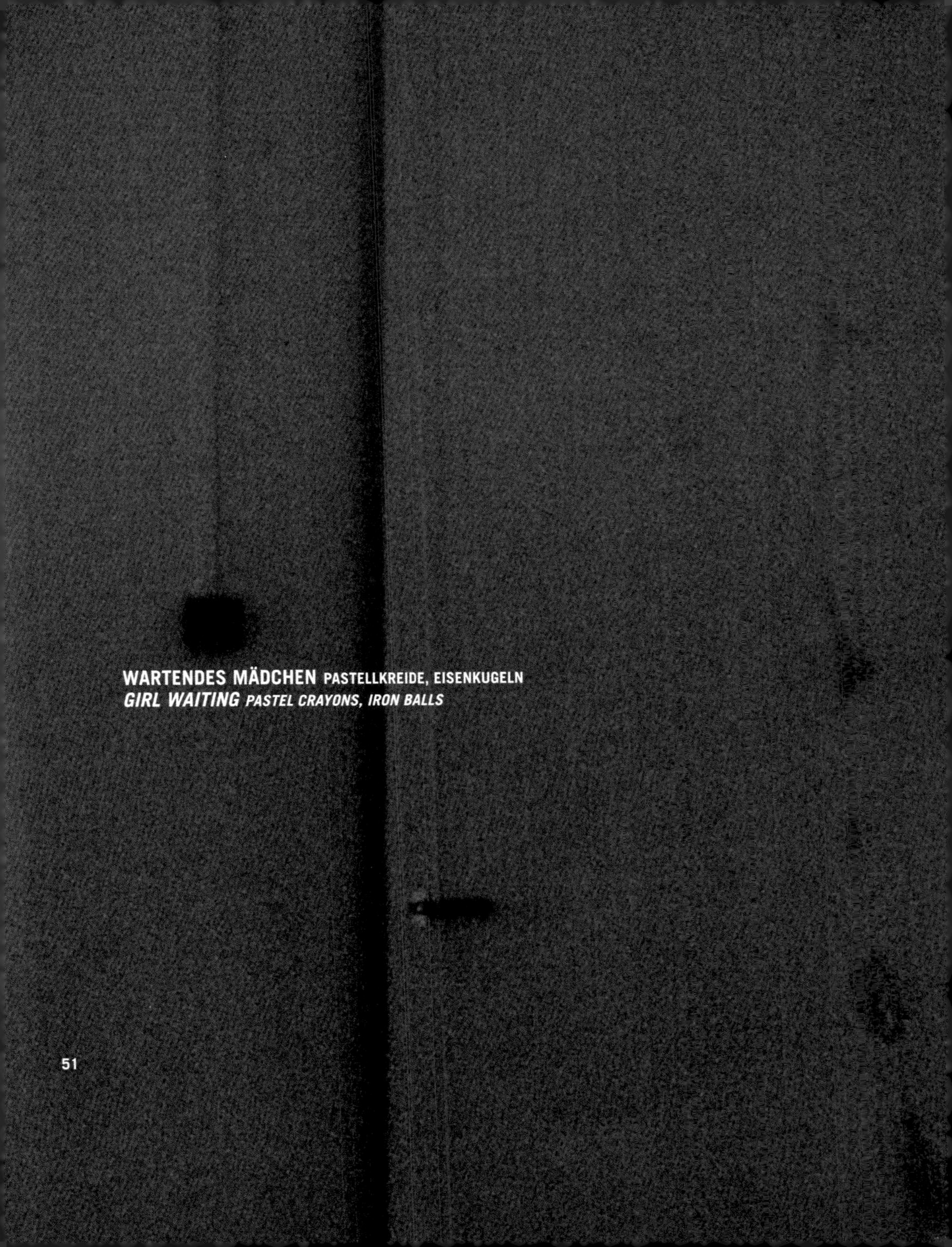

WARTENDES MÄDCHEN PASTELLKREIDE, EISENKUGELN
GIRL WAITING PASTEL CRAYONS, IRON BALLS

CHRISTOPH TANNERT #2 Ulrike Flaig hat einige anschauliche Beispiele dafür geliefert, auf welchen Schleichwegen der internen Problemerzeugungskapazität ihres Metiers man sich unbelastet vorwärtsbewegen kann. Zuerst fällt auf, dass die Künstlerin vollkommen frei zwischen verschiedenen Medien wechselt. Zeichnung, Fotografie, Video, Objektkunst, Installation und Sound-Erzeugung gelten ihr als gleichrangige Mittel. Sie schätzt die Laborpraktik mehr als ein endgültiges finito. Das verleiht all ihren ausgestellten Arbeiten eine Offenheit, die die Deutungsmöglichkeiten ständig (aber selbstverständlich nicht unendlich) erweitert. Hinzu kommt der Spaß am Sprachspiel in der Titelgebung, sodass häufig zwei unterschiedliche, einander bedingende Formalisierungsgrade eine Klammer bilden. Es mag verwundern, dass Ulrike Flaig oft mit armseligen Materialien arbeitet, die so gar nichts von der schnittigen, gelackten Oberflächenqualität unseres Zeitgeistes der Verführung haben. Spaß-Design, Glitter-Pop und Neurotischer Realismus handeln, wie wir wissen, mit Glasperlen und beleben das Showgeschäft. Aber diese Absage an den werbewirksamen schönen Schein kennzeichnet auch die Positionen anderer KünstlerInnen. Am Ende des Jahrzehnts der Hedonisten, der Leichtigkeit, Sorglosigkeit und Verantwortunglosigkeit zeigt sich deutlicher als vorher dessen andere Seite: die Lust am Einfachen, am Weggeworfenen und Improvisierten. *CHRISTOPH TANNERT #2 Ulrike Flaig has come up with a number of fine examples of the various yet unobstructed hidden paths of internal problem-creating potential that are available in her trade. The thing that is most striking is the fact that the artist freely switches from one medium to another. Drawings, photography, video, object art, installation and sound-production are all of equal importance to her. She prefers laboratory practice to the finite, and this results in a certain openness which consistently (but not infinitely, of course) extends the potentials of meaning in all her exhibited works. That and a certain playfulness in her titles, which she enjoys, more often than not leads to two different, interdependent degrees of formalisation providing a kind of bracket. It may surprise that Ulrike Flaig often uses shabby materials which do not all correspond to our glossy zeitgeist surface qualities. Fun design, glitter pop and neurotic realism only deal in glass beads, boosting show business, as we all know. But Ulrike Flaig is not the only artist foregoing high-gloss and commercially appealing appearances. At the end of a decade of hedonism, convenience, carelessness and irresponsibility, the other side of the coin is showing ever more clearly: the craving for the simple, the discarded, the improvised.*

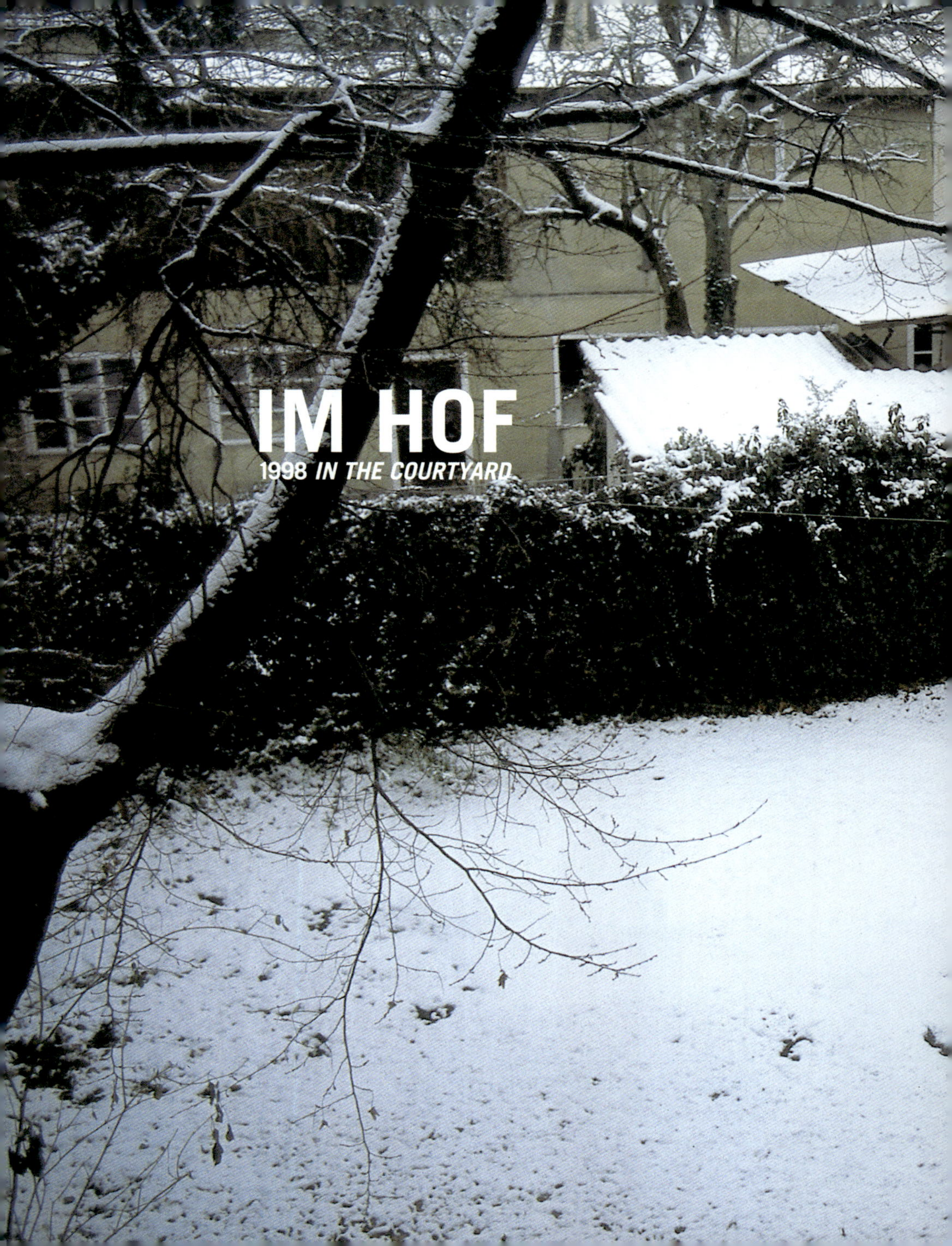
IM HOF
1998 IN THE COURTYARD

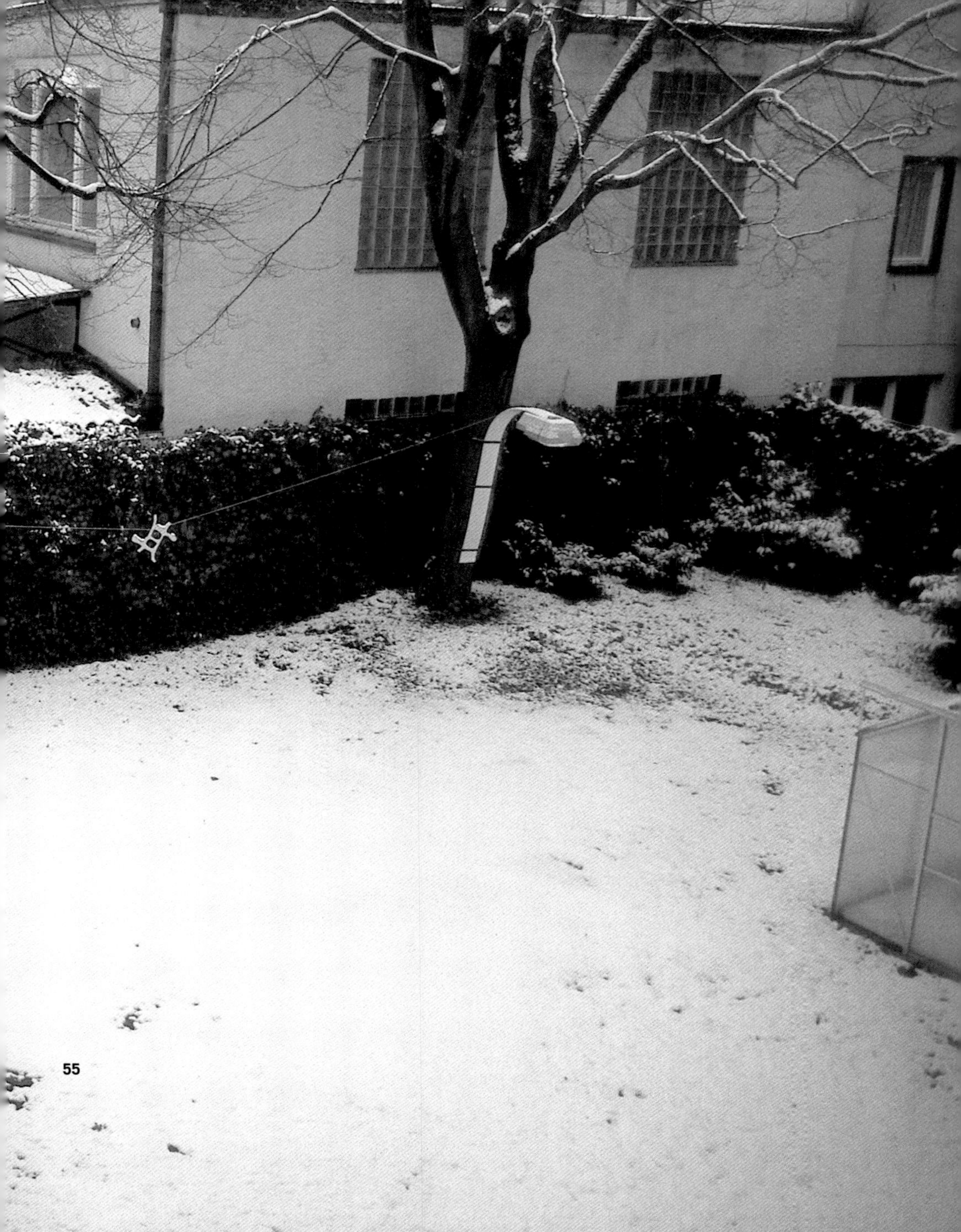

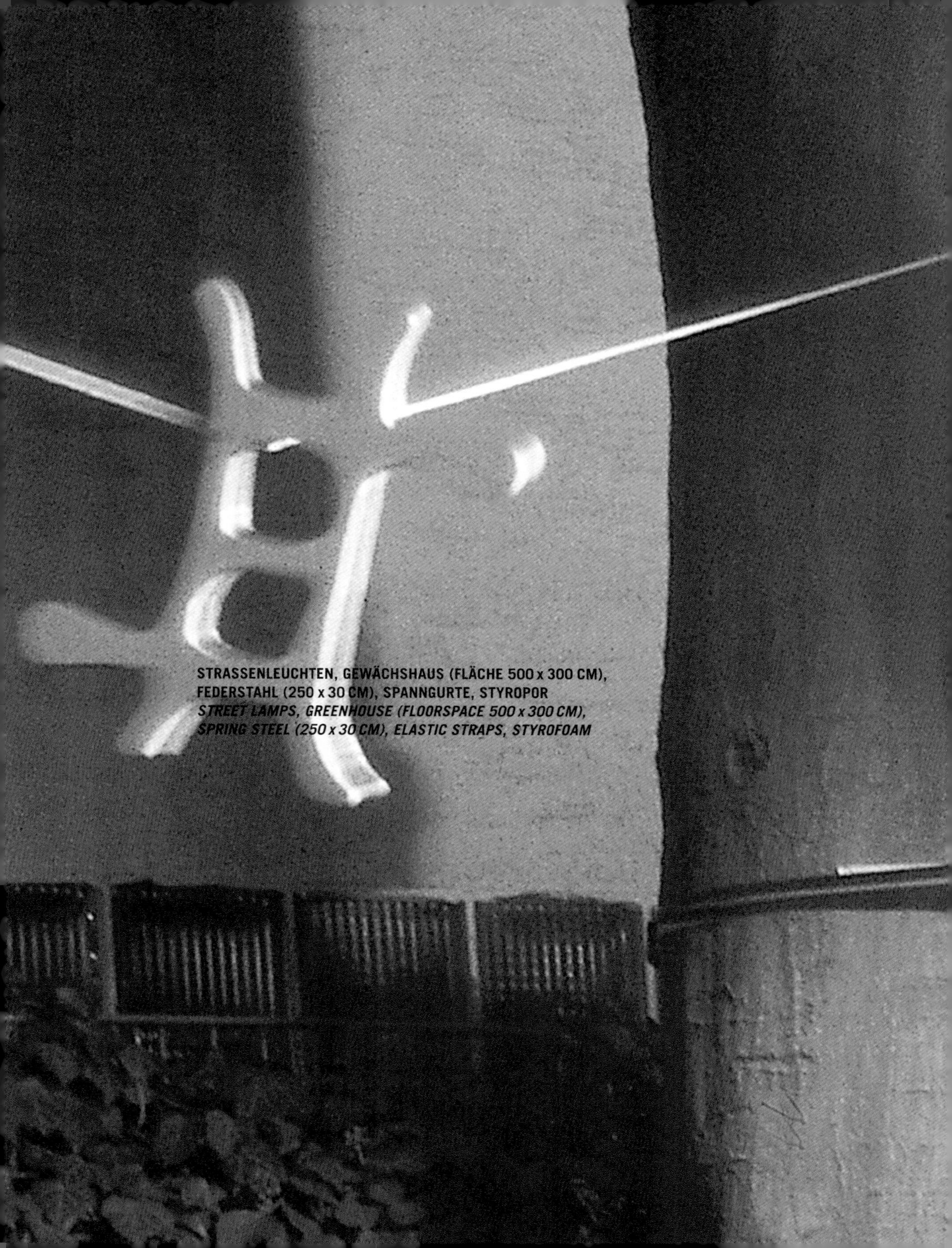

STRASSENLEUCHTEN, GEWÄCHSHAUS (FLÄCHE 500 x 300 CM),
FEDERSTAHL (250 x 30 CM), SPANNGURTE, STYROPOR
STREET LAMPS, GREENHOUSE (FLOORSPACE 500 x 300 CM),
SPRING STEEL (250 x 30 CM), ELASTIC STRAPS, STYROFOAM

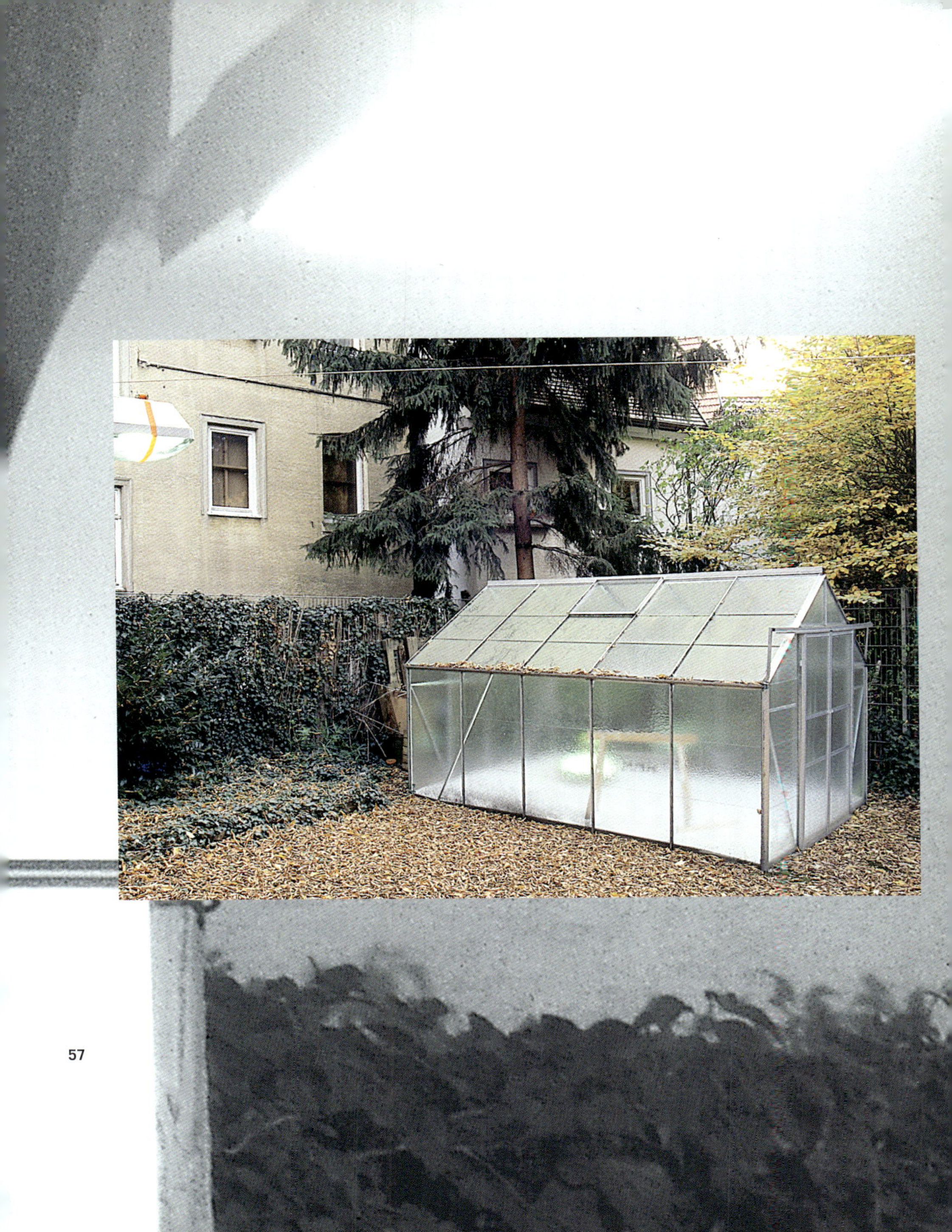

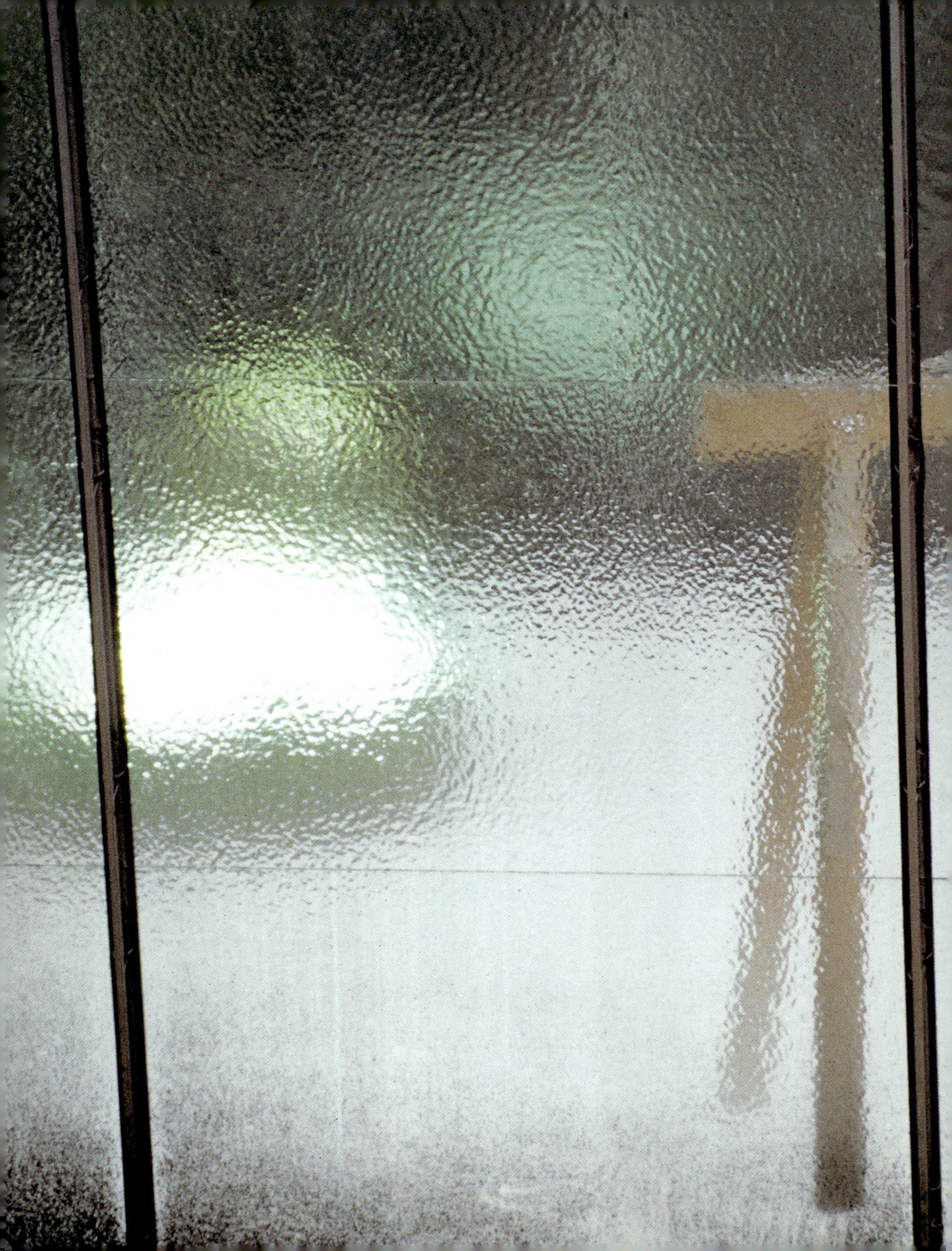

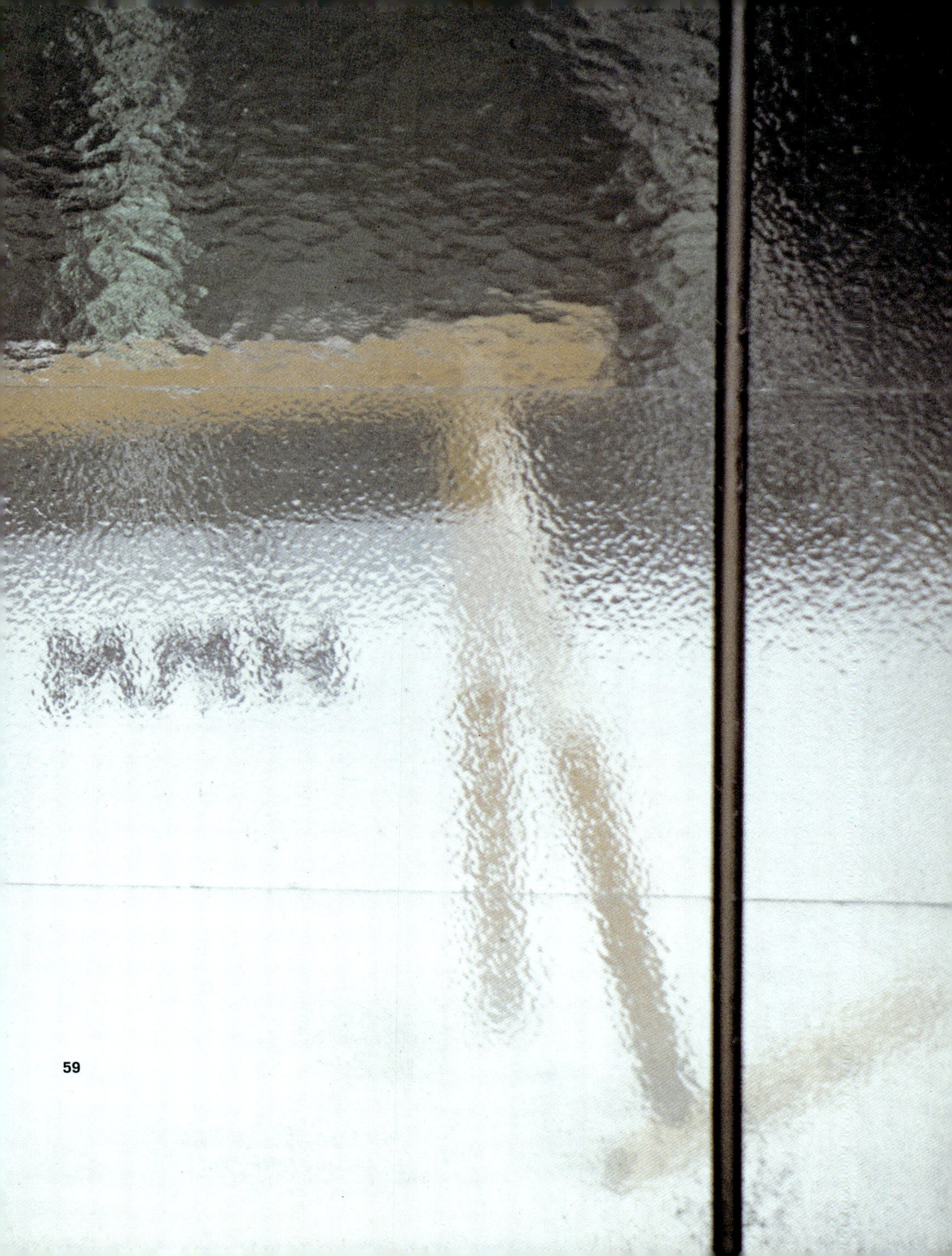

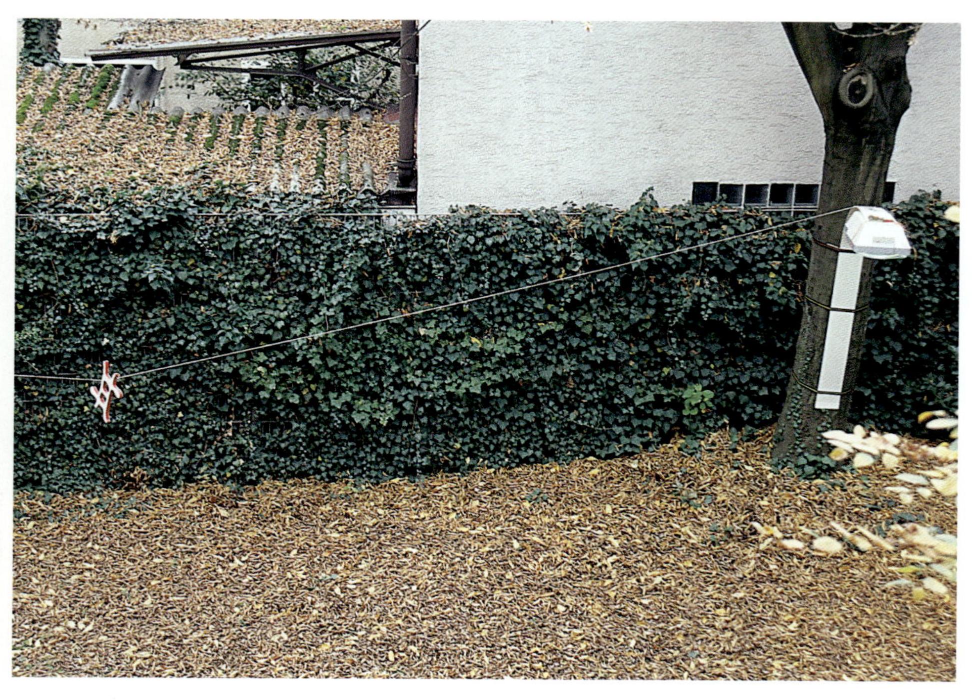

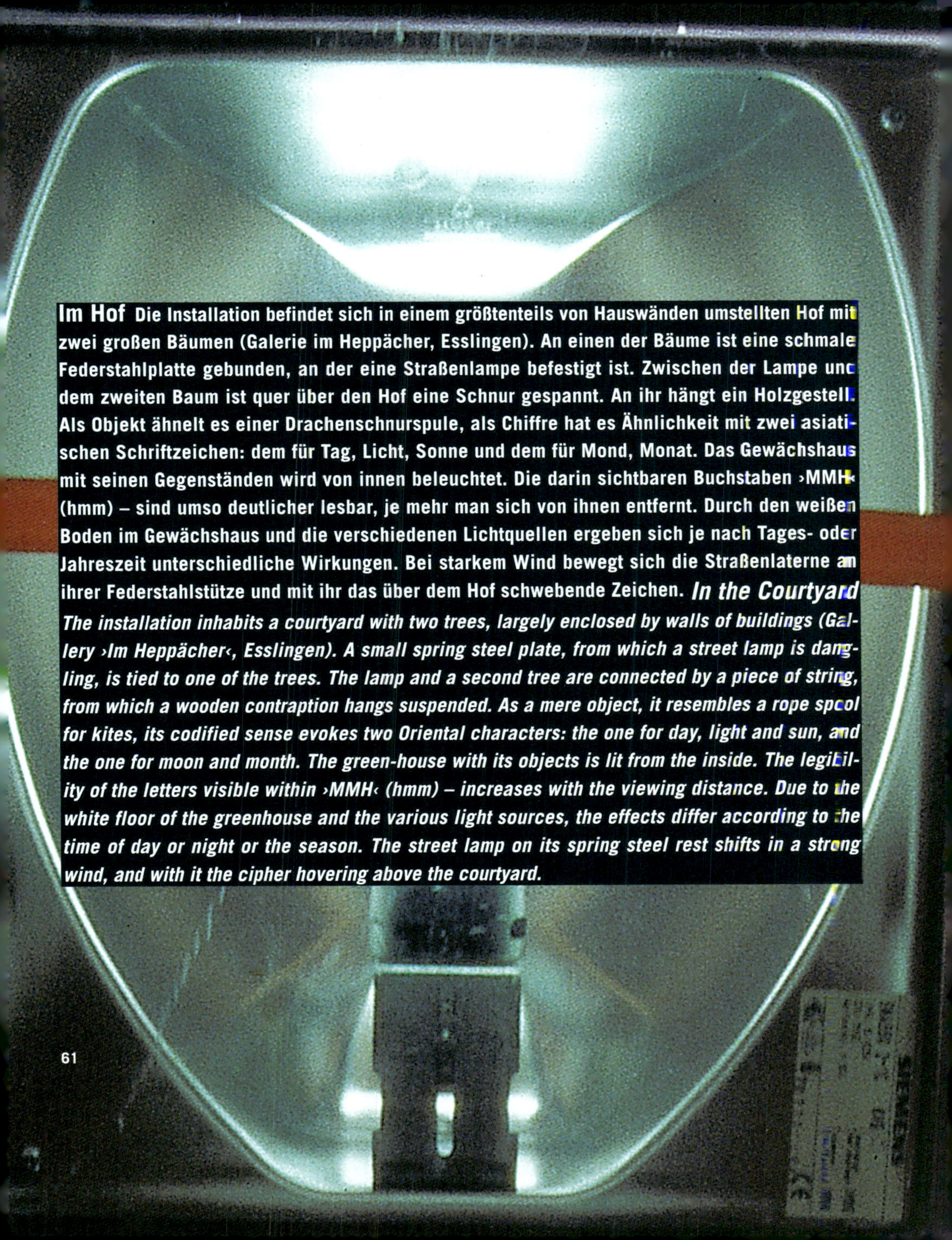

Im Hof Die Installation befindet sich in einem größtenteils von Hauswänden umstellten Hof mit zwei großen Bäumen (Galerie im Heppächer, Esslingen). An einen der Bäume ist eine schmale Federstahlplatte gebunden, an der eine Straßenlampe befestigt ist. Zwischen der Lampe und dem zweiten Baum ist quer über den Hof eine Schnur gespannt. An ihr hängt ein Holzgestell. Als Objekt ähnelt es einer Drachenschnurspule, als Chiffre hat es Ähnlichkeit mit zwei asiatischen Schriftzeichen: dem für Tag, Licht, Sonne und dem für Mond, Monat. Das Gewächshaus mit seinen Gegenständen wird von innen beleuchtet. Die darin sichtbaren Buchstaben ›MMH‹ (hmm) – sind umso deutlicher lesbar, je mehr man sich von ihnen entfernt. Durch den weißen Boden im Gewächshaus und die verschiedenen Lichtquellen ergeben sich je nach Tages- oder Jahreszeit unterschiedliche Wirkungen. Bei starkem Wind bewegt sich die Straßenlaterne an ihrer Federstahlstütze und mit ihr das über dem Hof schwebende Zeichen. *In the Courtyard*

The installation inhabits a courtyard with two trees, largely enclosed by walls of buildings (Gallery ›Im Heppächer‹, Esslingen). A small spring steel plate, from which a street lamp is dangling, is tied to one of the trees. The lamp and a second tree are connected by a piece of string, from which a wooden contraption hangs suspended. As a mere object, it resembles a rope spool for kites, its codified sense evokes two Oriental characters: the one for day, light and sun, and the one for moon and month. The green-house with its objects is lit from the inside. The legibility of the letters visible within ›MMH‹ (hmm) – increases with the viewing distance. Due to the white floor of the greenhouse and the various light sources, the effects differ according to the time of day or night or the season. The street lamp on its spring steel rest shifts in a strong wind, and with it the cipher hovering above the courtyard.

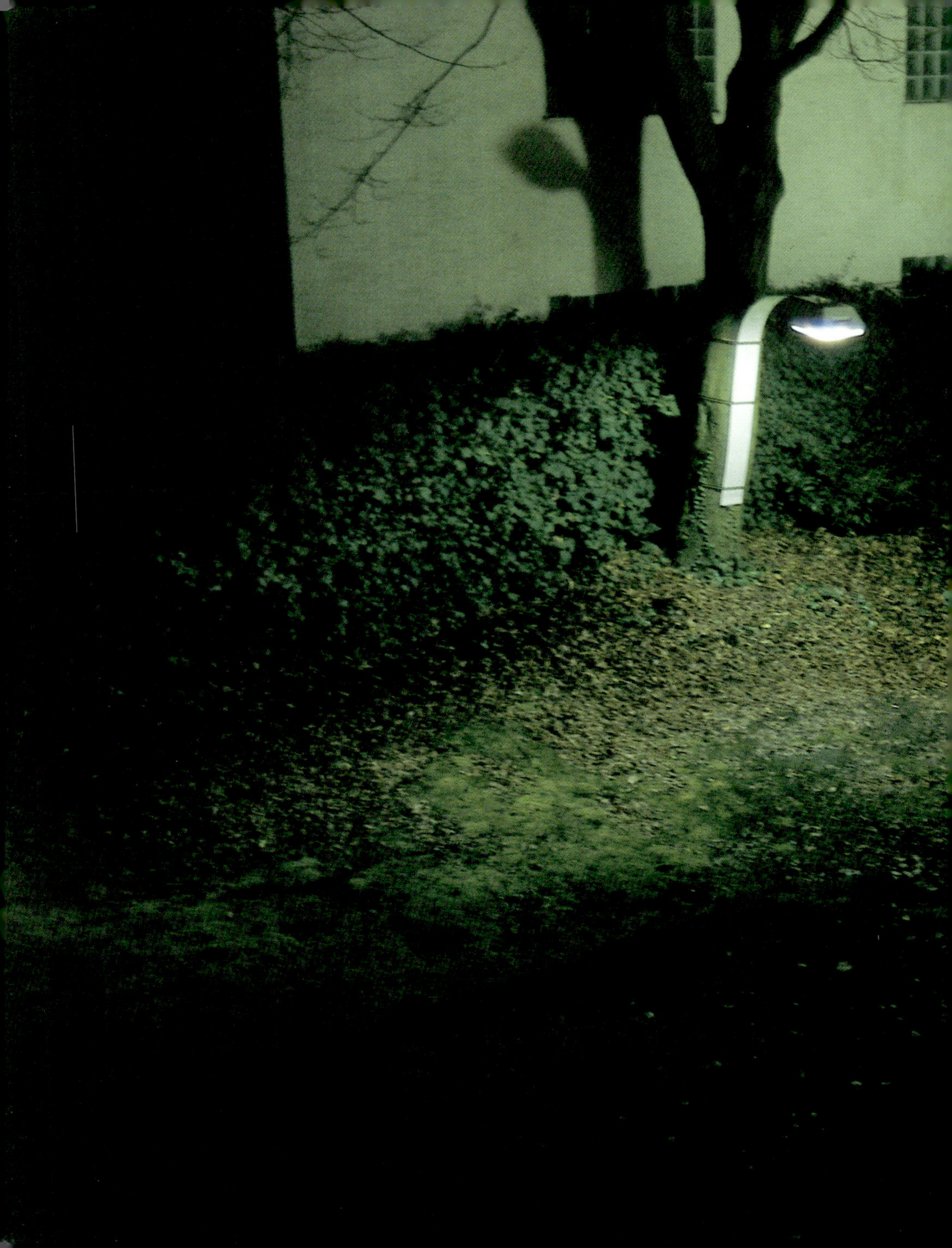

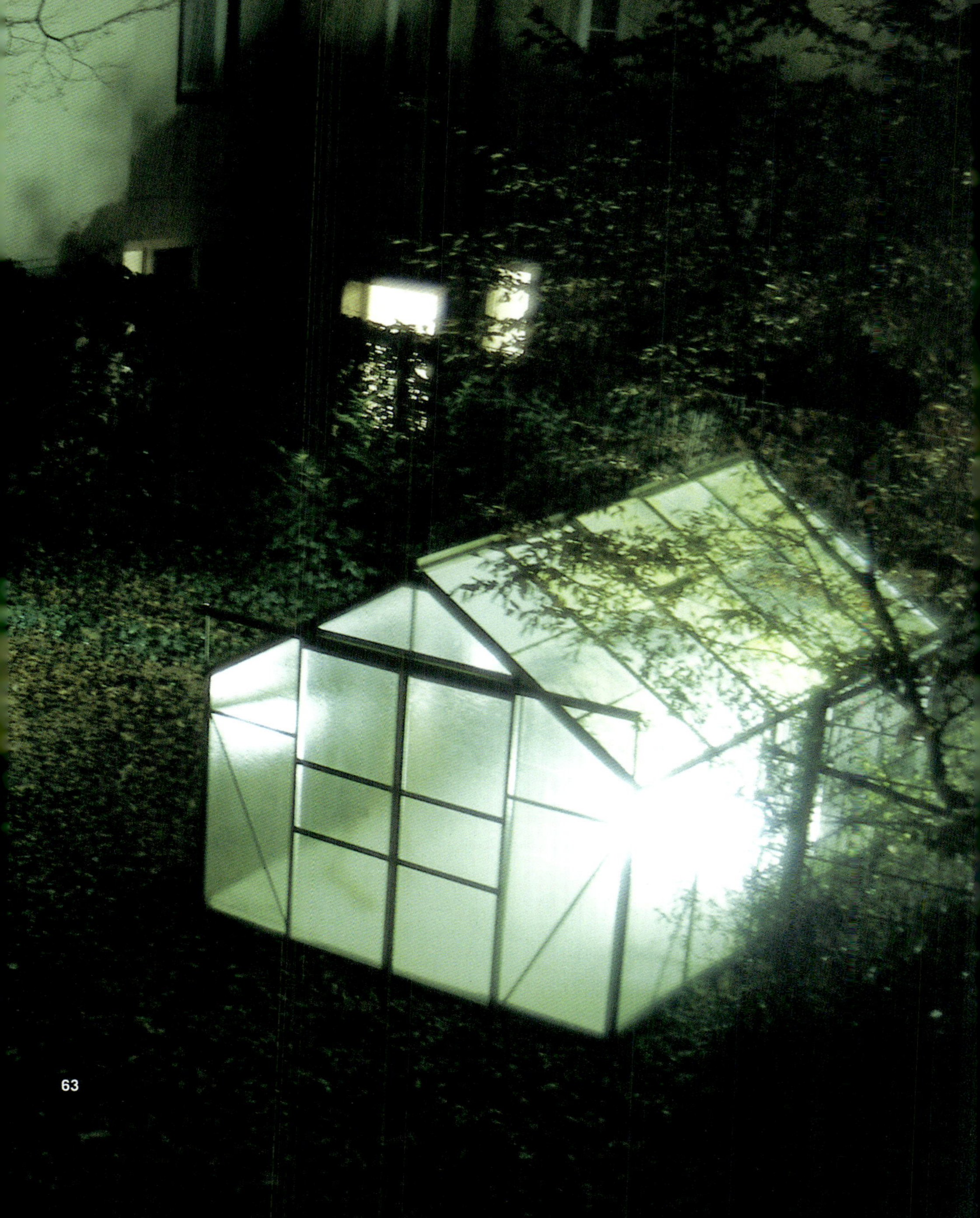

CHRISTOPH TANNERT #3 Unverwechselbar sind die Werke von Ulrike Flaig immer dann, wenn sie einfach sind – die pure Präsenz der Substanz. ›Dann wird die Sprache intensiv, ein reines Kontinuum von Werten und Intensitäten. Dann wird jede Sprache geheim und hat dennoch nichts zu verbergen, dann braucht man kein geheimes Subsystem innerhalb der Sprache auszutüfteln. Zu diesem Ergebnis kommt man nur durch Nüchternheit, durch schöpferische Abstraktion‹ – so haben es Gilles Deleuze und Félix Guattari in ›Mille plateaux‹ treffend formuliert.[1] Das einfach Seiende wächst sich beim Sampling naturgemäß zum Komplexen aus, weil die künstlerischen, medialen, technischen und sozialen Einsprengsel unterschiedlichster Herkunft, von Ulrike Flaig konzentriert und präzise verknüpft, ein neues Netz an Konnotationen entstehen lassen. Die Unendlichkeit ineinander verschachtelter Universen des Cyberspace ist nach wie vor ein Anziehungspunkt für Wanderer, die sich grenzenlos ergehen wollen. Der Traum von den unbegrenzten Möglichkeiten hat sich ins Virtuelle verlagert, doch im Bereich der realen, tastbaren Welt kehrt ein gesunder Pessimismus zurück. Dass die Simulation sich anschickt, ihre Schöpfer zu fressen, werden diese, selbst wenn sie außerhalb der Simulation leben oder sich in anderen Bereichen des Netzes tummeln, bald schon erfahren. Einen Materialmix aus Zuckerguss, Draht, Papier, Nylon, Styropor, Gips, Holz, Pressspan, Glas, Knetgummi, Kaugummi und diversen Fundstücken zu sehen, zu riechen und anzufassen, kann einen Rezipienten durchaus auf neue Art und Weise sinnlichleibhaftig sesshaft machen. Die gegenteilige Erfahrung wäre: als Geisel einer Playstation im Rausch der Bilder zerfasert zu werden. *CHRISTOPH TANNERT #3 Ulrike Flaig's works are always unmistakable when they simply are – the pure presence of substance. ›Then the language intensifies, a pure continuum of values and intensities. Then every language becomes a secret one, without hiding anything, then no secret subsystem within the language is needed. This may only be achieved by sobriety, by creative abstraction‹ – as Gilles Deleuze and Félix Guattari aptly observed in ›Mille plateaux‹.[1] With sampling, that which simply is naturally grows into something complex, since the artistic, medial, technical and social inclusions from various origins, concentrated and carefully interconnected by Ulrike Flaig, create their own network of connotations. While the maze of interrelated universes of cyberspace continues to attract wanderers longing for the borderless, and the dream of unlimited possibilities has shifted to the virtual, in the area of the real, the palpable, a healthy pessimism has returned. That the simulation is about to devour its creators will soon reveal itself also to them, even if they* *exist outside of the simulation or are busy elsewhere in the net. To smell and touch a mixture of materials of frosting, wire, paper, nylon, Styrofoam, plaster, pressboard, glass, play dough, chewing gum and various found objects may well provide the recipient, actually and sensually, with new grounding. The alternative would be to decompose slowly in a rush of pictures while being held hostage by a play station.*

[1] Gilles Deleuze und / *and* Félix Guattari, Tausend Plateaus, Berlin 1992, Seite / *page* 137

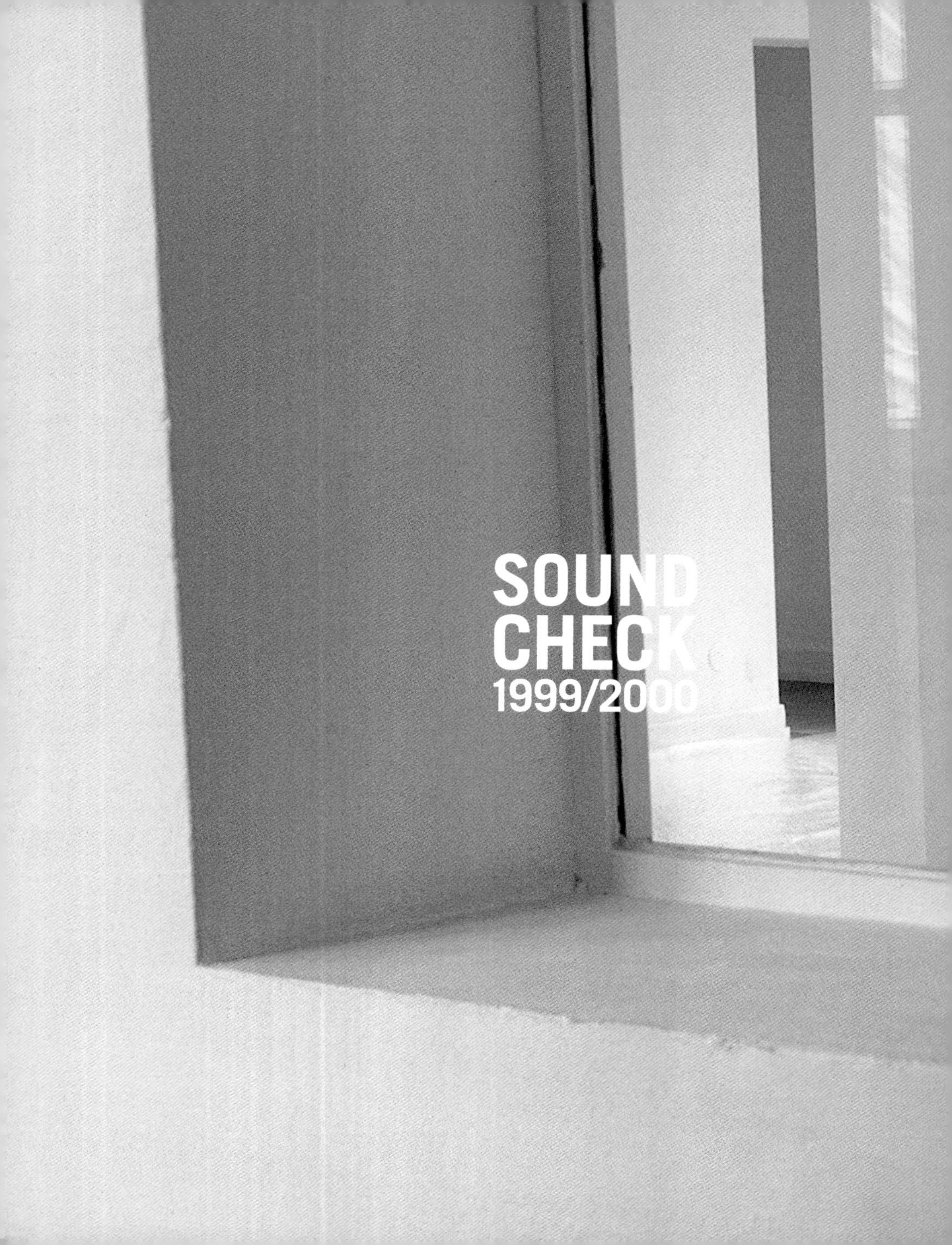

SOUND
CHECK
1999/2000

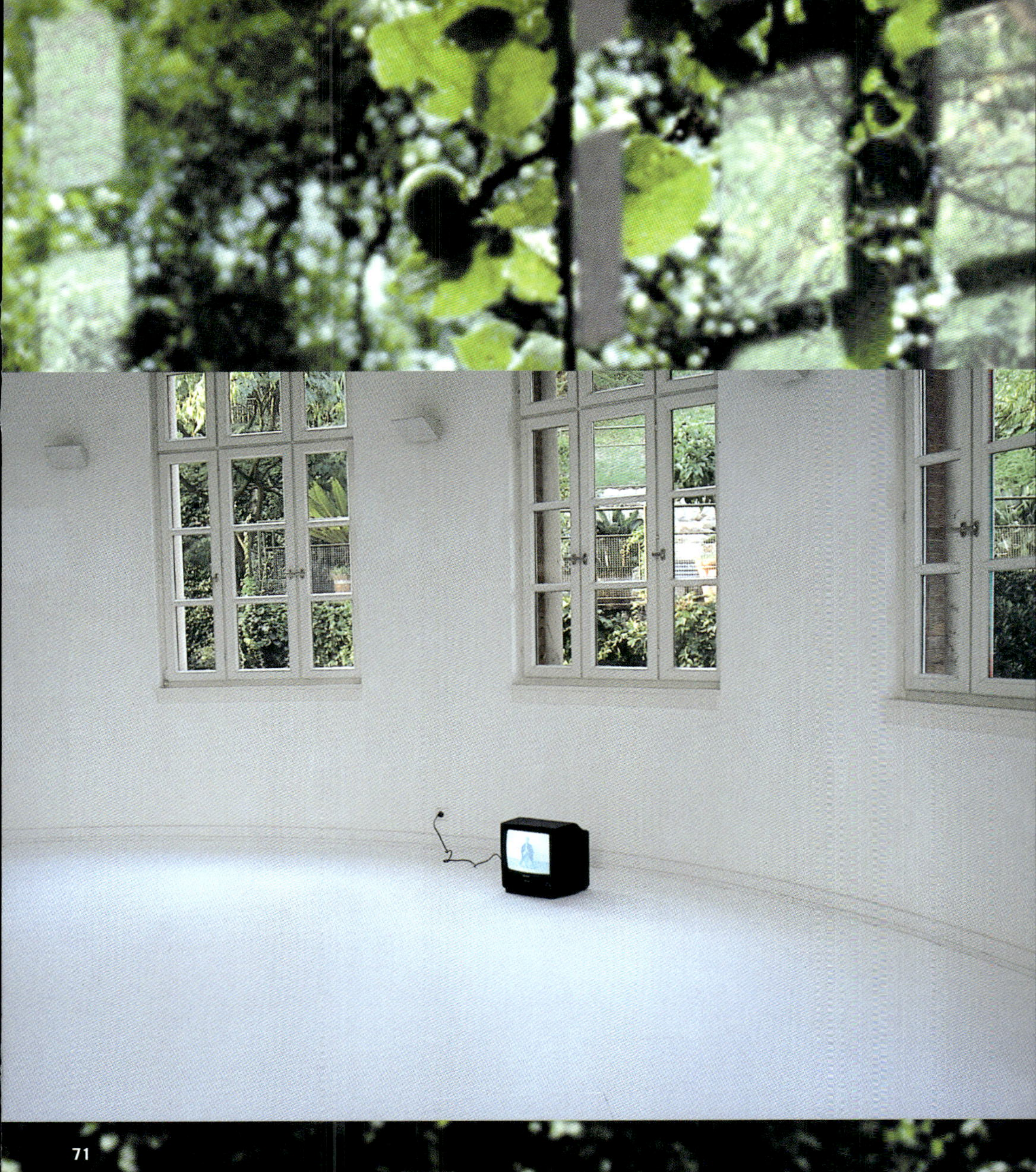

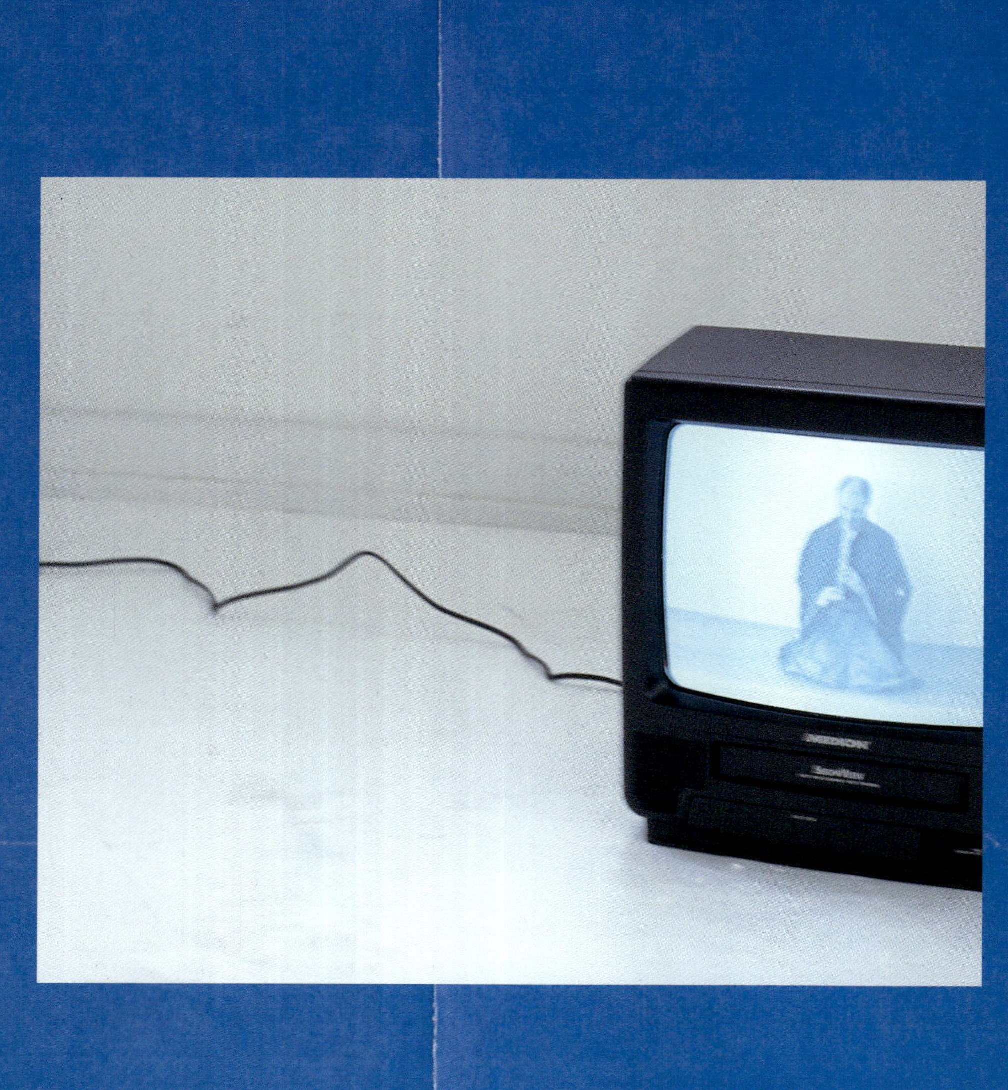

Soundcheck (Gesellschaft der Freunde Junger Kunst, Baden-Baden) Die Arbeit umfasst drei Räume: Im ersten Raum ist ein leises, ostinates Bleistiftgeräusch zu hören. Das Video zeigt den Musiker und Komponisten Jim Franklin, eine Shakuhachi-Flöte spielend. Auf der gegenüberliegenden Wand verläuft ein vertikaler Bleistiftstrich von der Decke bis zum Boden. Beide Geräusche im Raum sind so leise, dass die Schritte des Besuchers auf dem Styropor immer den akustischen Gesamteindruck dominieren. Beim Betreten des zweiten Raumes knackt der Bodenbelag – eine Luftpolsterfolie. Die Nummer des auf dem Sockel montierten Mobiltelefons ist auf kleinen, dort ausgelegten Flyern abgedruckt und erlaubt es, sich nach dem Ausstellungsbesuch akustisch in Erinnerung zu bringen oder gar zu kommunizieren. Im dritten Raum ist die Arbeitssituation für die Performance ›Watching Music‹ aufgebaut. In Abwesenheit der Akteure zeigt die dort installierte Videoprojektion permanent die Ton-Bild-Sequenz, in der ein Camcorder live als Instrument eingesetzt wurde. *Soundcheck (Gesellschaft der Freunde Junger Kunst, Baden-Baden) The piece consists of three rooms: In the first room, a soft, persistent noise from a pencil is heard. The video shows the musician and composer Jim Franklin playing a Shakuhachi flute. On the opposite wall, a vertical pencil line extends from the ceiling to the floor. Both sounds in the room are so soft that the acoustic impression of the whole is dominated by the visitors' steps on the Styrofoam. Upon entering the second room, the floor covering – bubble wrap – pops under the visitors' steps. The number of the cellular phone permanently fixed on the plinth is printed on a stack of small flyers beside it, allowing visitors to make an acoustic entry or even to communicate after leaving the exhibition. The third room contains the set for the performance ›Watching Music‹. In absence of the actors, the video projection installed there continously shows the sound-picture-sequence, in which a camcorder was being used live as an instrument.*

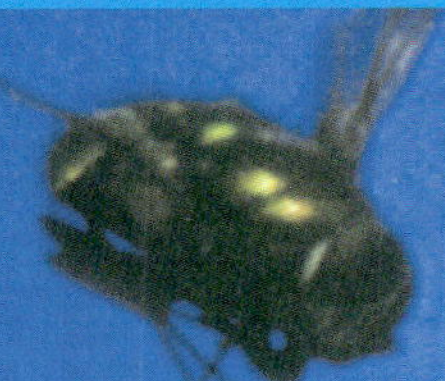

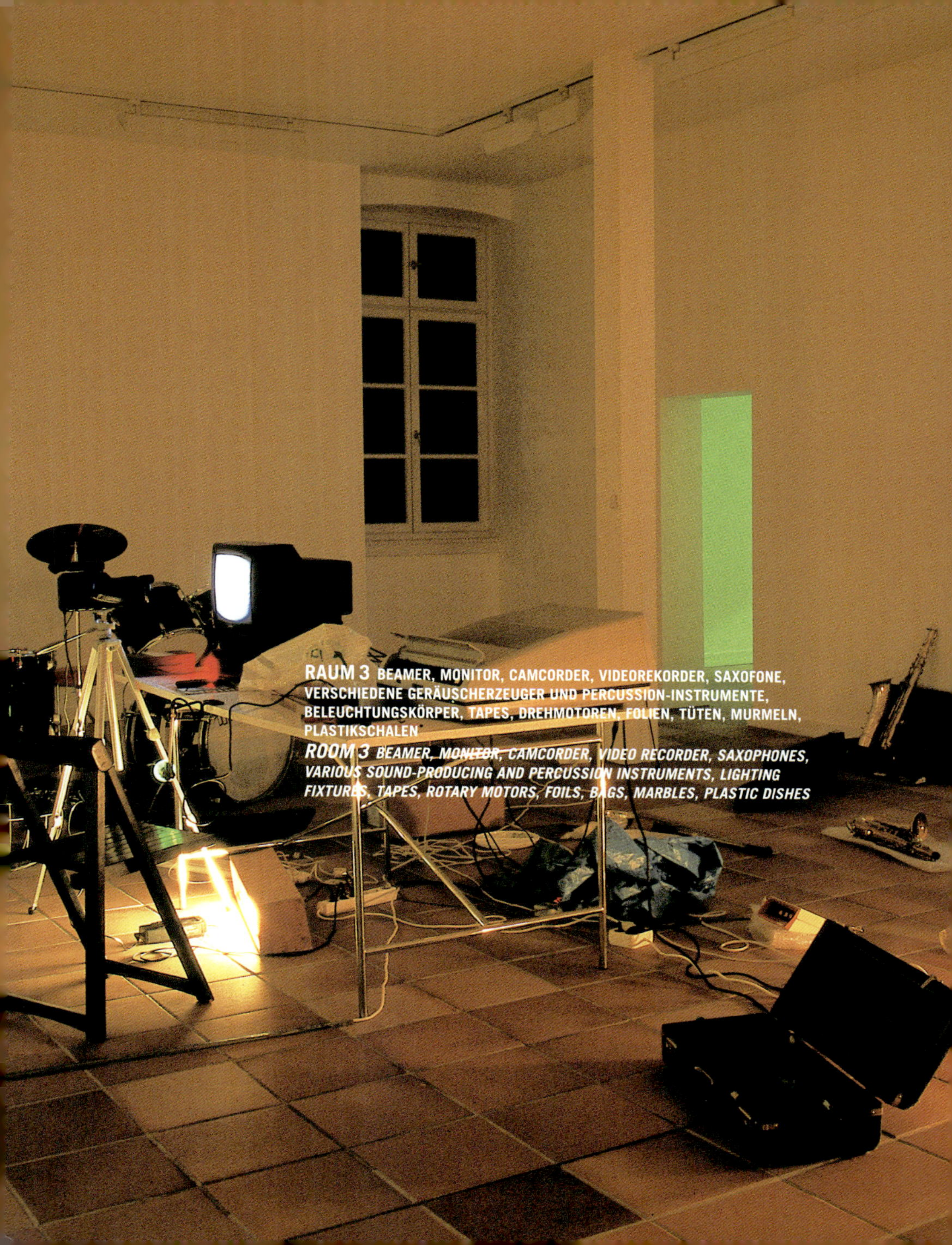

RAUM 3 BEAMER, MONITOR, CAMCORDER, VIDEOREKORDER, SAXOFONE, VERSCHIEDENE GERÄUSCHERZEUGER UND PERCUSSION-INSTRUMENTE, BELEUCHTUNGSKÖRPER, TAPES, DREHMOTOREN, FOLIEN, TÜTEN, MURMELN, PLASTIKSCHALEN

ROOM 3 BEAMER, MONITOR, CAMCORDER, VIDEO RECORDER, SAXOPHONES, VARIOUS SOUND-PRODUCING AND PERCUSSION INSTRUMENTS, LIGHTING FIXTURES, TAPES, ROTARY MOTORS, FOILS, BAGS, MARBLES, PLASTIC DISHES

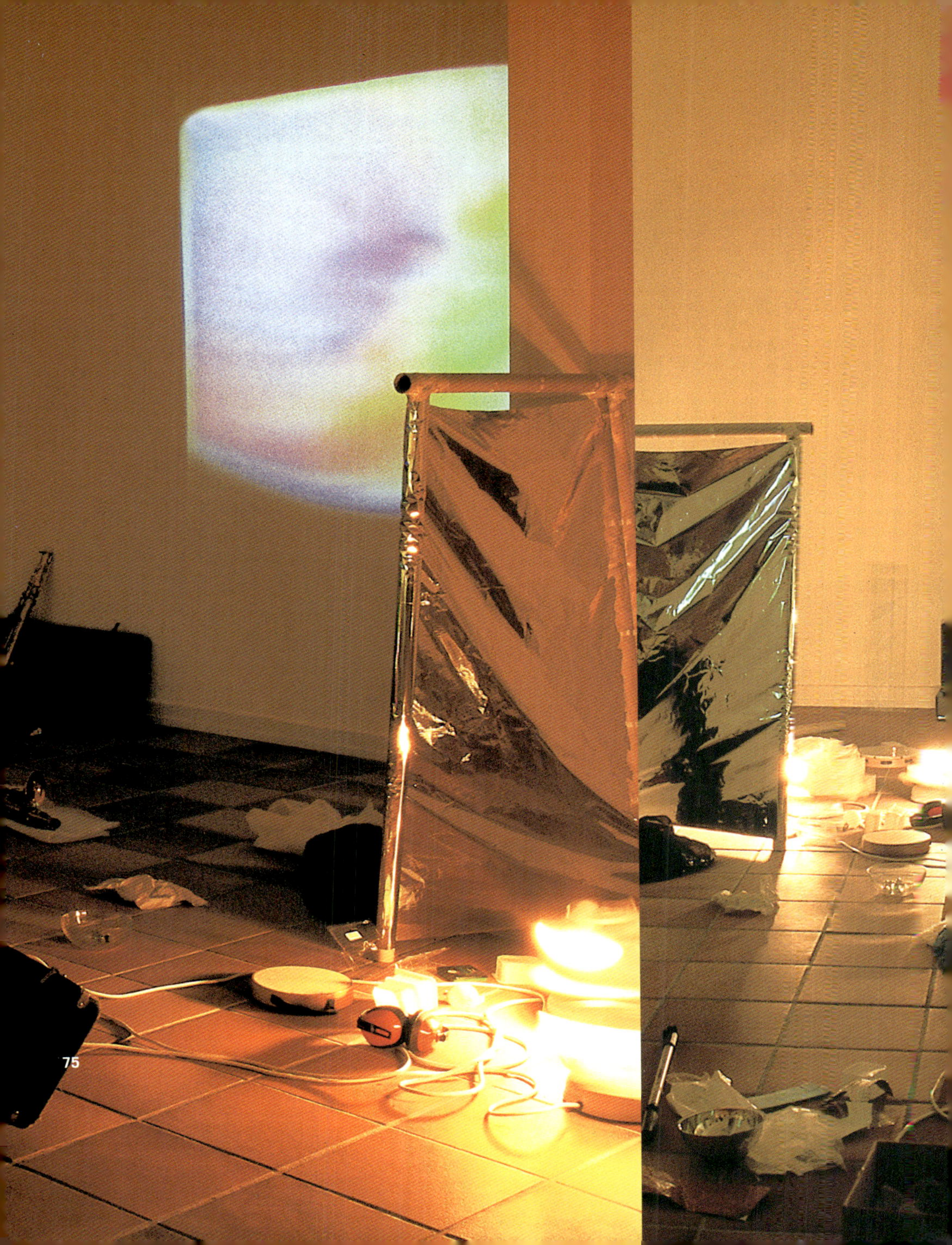

75

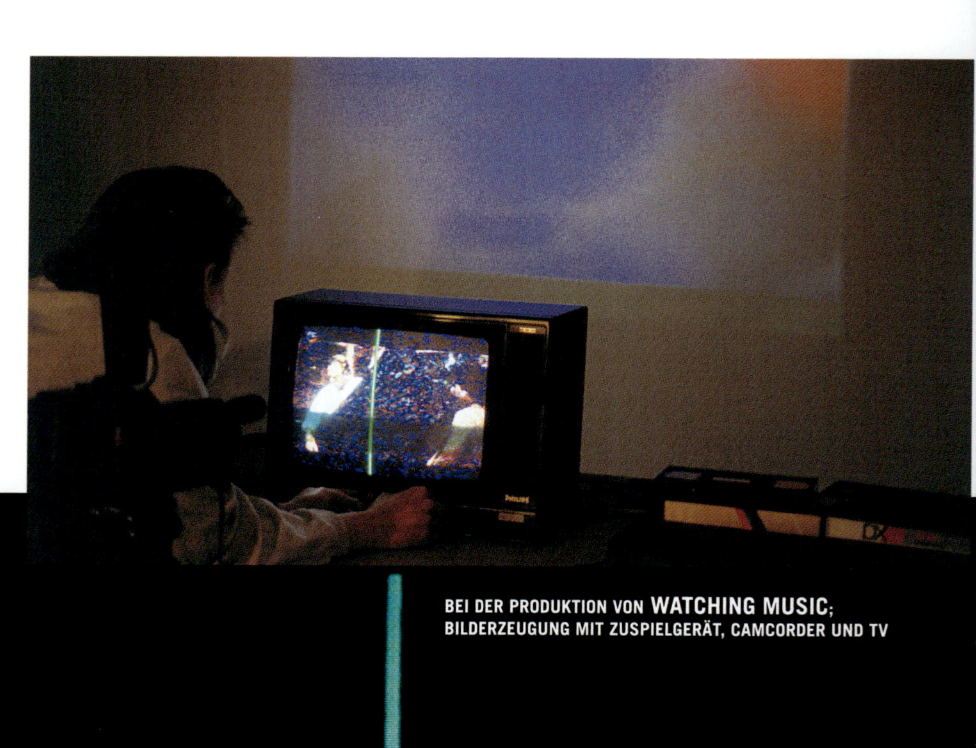

BEI DER PRODUKTION VON **WATCHING MUSIC**;
BILDERZEUGUNG MIT ZUSPIELGERÄT, CAMCORDER UND TV

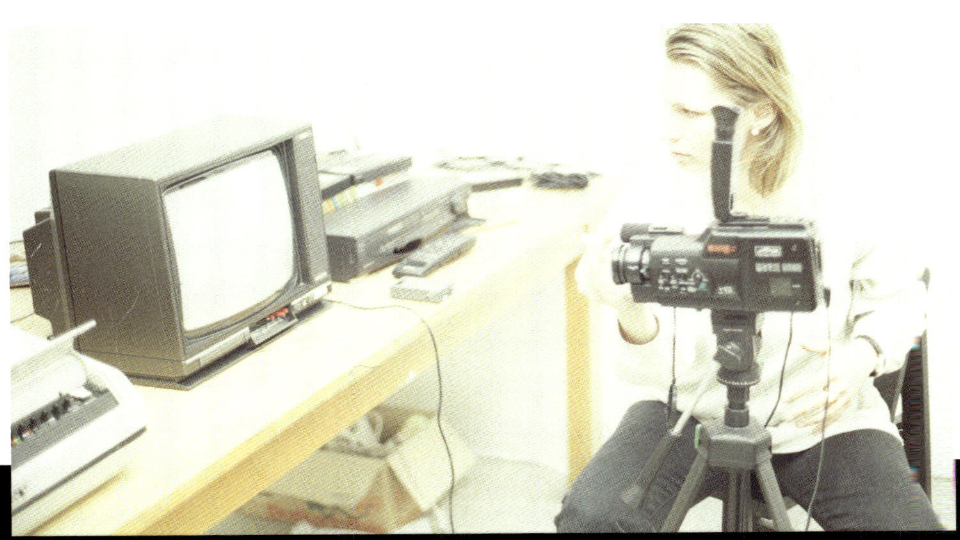

AT THE PRODUCTION OF WATCHING MUSIC; IMAGE
GENERATION WITH VIDEO RECORDER, CAMCORDER AND TV

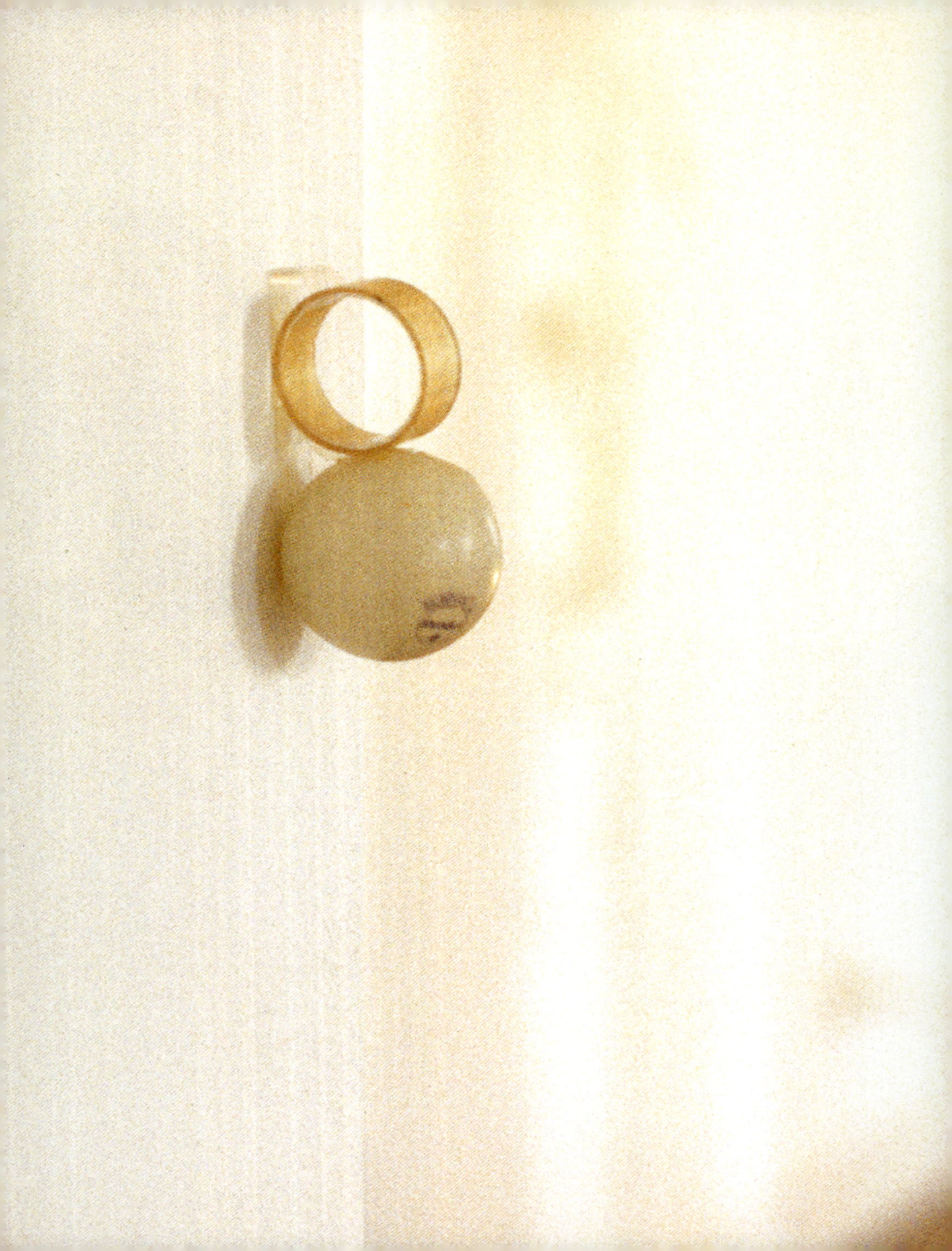

TEIL NR. 8 TESAFILMROLLE, TISCHTENNISBALL, 3 x 3 x 6 CM
PART NO. 8 ROLL OF SCOTCH TAPE, TABLE TENNIS BALL, 3 x 3 x 6 CM

CHRISTOPH TANNERT #4 Ulrike Flaigs scheinbar zusammengewürfelte Materialverkettungen haben mehr verstörende Kraft als die allgegenwärtige Philisteraufgeklärtheit. Aus Einzelteilen setzt die Künstlerin das Ungewisse zusammen, jagt das Ganzheitliche in die Luft, um den Eigenheiten der Schöpfung auf die Spur zu kommen. Auf nichts reagiert sie so empfindlich wie auf falsche Harmonie. So sind bei ihr Präsenz und Polyvalenz die Anfangs- und Endpunkte derselben Variationslinie. Das betrifft auch ihre Auffassung in Bezug auf einen gendertheoretischen Blick, auf Körperbewusstsein, Macht- und Abhängigkeitsstrukturen. Die Lesart, die Ulrike Flaig beispielsweise in ›Lady‹ (1995), ›Frauen und Technik‹ (1995) oder in ›Die Tapferkeit oder das Stärkersein als man selbst‹ (1997) vorgibt, reproduziert weder die alten Ideologeme noch berauscht sie sich an Körperphantasmen, sie ist weder symbolisch noch illusionistisch noch analytisch. Stattdessen stehen die Objektarrangements wie Schattenkörper im Raum herum und zeigen nichts als ihre Disparatheit. Die Kargheit der Ausstattung und ein konzentrierter Formwille markieren das Gegenteil eines Glaubenssystems. Ulrike Flaig denkt in strukturalen und strukturierenden Organisationsformen. Das macht das Eigenleben und die Widerspenstigkeit ihrer Werke aus, die weniger Vehikel der Identitätsfindung sind als vielmehr Partikel in einem Atomisierungsprozess. Indem sie den Eindruck des Zufälligen vermeidet und gleichzeitig überzeugend das Gefühl von Unordnung innerhalb des Systems vermittelt, schafft die Künstlerin nichtsdestoweniger ein politisches Koordinatensystem, das sich dem Autoritären in jeglicher Spielart entgegensetzt. Für einen angemessenen Zugang zu den Werken von Ulrike Flaig ist es wichtig, sich dieser Rahmenbedingungen bewusst zu werden. Und doch können Analysen bei der Betrachtung nur eine Hilfestellung geben. Auf das mediale Äußerungsgefüge und den Reichtum kontinuierlicher Variation muss man sich einfach mit allen Sinnen einlassen. Wenn sich das Unerwartete ereignen soll, müssen sich die Betrachter in der Substanz der Werke befinden – dort, wo es atmet, fließt, sich bewegt, blinkt, sich spiegelt, wo Bilder und Geräusche erzeugt werden, kurz: Dort, wo das ›Noch-nicht-Determinierte‹ seinen Schwebezustand auskostet.

CHRISTOPH TANNERT #4 Ulrike Flaig's seemingly randomly linked materials have more disturbing power than the omnipresent philistine enlightenment of today. The artist assembles the tentative from individual parts, blows the allencompassing sky-high in order to find the peculiarities of creation. She cannot abide false harmonies. In her work, presence and polyvalence are the starting and ending points of one and the same line of variation. This also concerns her ideas with respect to gender-theoretical approaches, to body consciousness, structures of power and dependence. The readings presented by Ulrike Flaig in ›Lady‹ (1995), ›Women and Technology‹ (1995) and ›Braveness or Being Stronger than Oneself‹ (1997), for example, neither reproduce old ideologies nor do they delude themselves with physical fancies, they are neither symbolic, nor illusionistic nor analytical. Rather, the arrangements of objects occupy their space like spectres, showing nothing but disparity. The sparseness of the resources and a concentrated will of form delineate the opposite of dogma. Ulrike Flaig thinks in structural and structuring forms of organization. And this is what characterizes the independence and the willfulness of her works, which are much less vehicles in a search for identity but more so particles in a process of atomization. And yet, avoiding the impression of the accidental but at the same time convincingly conveying the feeling of disorder within the system, the artist succeeds in creating a political system of coordinates that resists authoritarianism in every guise. For an adequate access to Ulrike Flaig's works, it is important to know the general framework of her art. Still, analyses can only be of small help to the observer, who must simply yield – with all senses – to the medial structure of expression and the wealth of continuous variation. If the unexpected is to happen, observers must find themselves in the substance of her works – there where the breathing, pulsating, moving, blinking and reflecting occurs, where pictures and sounds are produced, in short: where the ›not-yet-determined‹ is revelling in its state of suspense.

AUSWAHL AN ARBEITEN AUS DEN JAHREN 1989 BIS 1997
SELECTED WORKS FROM THE YEARS 1989 TO 1997

#1 **Thema Einhorn I, 1989/90** Installation mit zwei Monitoren, die zeitgleich auf zwei 30-minütigen Videofilmen kurze Szenen mit mehreren Schauspielern zeigen. Die elektronische Musik für das Video arrangierte der Komponist Jim Franklin. *Topic Unicorn I, 1989/90 Installation with two monitors, which simultaneously show two 30-minute videos with short scenes starring several actors. The electronic music for the video was composed by Jim Franklin.*

#2 **Hände und Füße, 1991** Zuckerguss, Schwarzweißfoto, Draht. Der Glukosegehalt wurde so dosiert, dass die Formen sich allmählich auflösen und eine Zuckerlache am Boden bilden. *Hands and Feet, 1991 frosting, black-and-white photograph, wire. The glucose content of the frosting is such that the shapes gradually dissolve forming a sugar water puddle on the floor.*

#3 **Hommage an Stuttgart, 1992/93** Luftballon, Super-8-Filmprojektion (Endlosschleife), Filmprojektor, Hocker. Ein halbtransparenter Luftballon hängt an einem Bindfaden im Raum. Der Film ist speziell auf die dreidimensionale Projektionsfläche abgestimmt. *Homage à Stuttgart, 1992/93 balloon, Super-8-film projection (infinite loop), film projector, stool. A semitransparent balloon is suspended in the room on a thread. The film has been especially tailored to the three-dimensional projection surface.*

#4 **Würden Sie uns bitte eine Szene aus einem Film erzählen, an die Sie sich erinnern?, 1993** mit Astrid S. Klein, Videoinstallation im Foyer des Gloria-Kinos in Geislingen. Passanten wurden aufgefordert, Filmszenen nachzuerzählen. Diese Interviews sind mit kurzen Sequenzen kombiniert, die zum Beispiel Hände in Aktion zeigen. *Would you please tell us a scene from a film that you remember?, 1993 with Astrid S. Klein, video installation in the foyer of the Gloria movie theater at Geislingen. Passers-by were asked to retell scenes from a movie. These interviews are combined with short sequences which, for instance, show hands in action.*

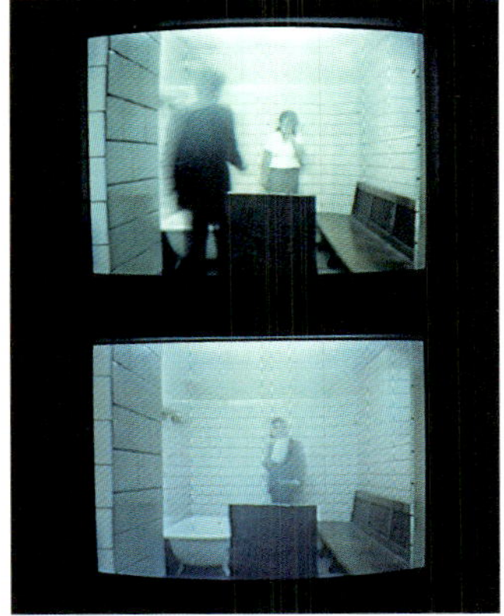

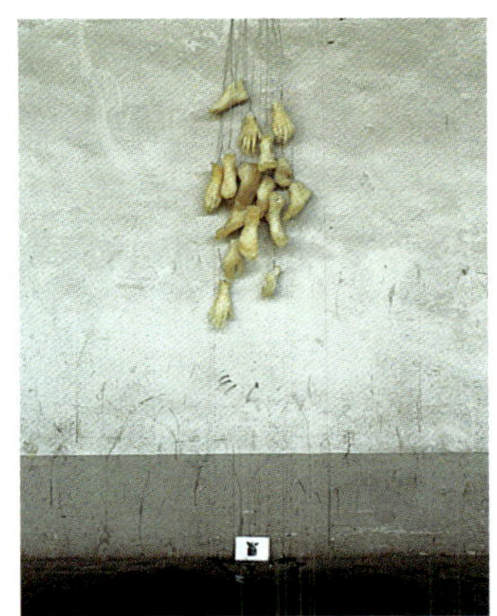

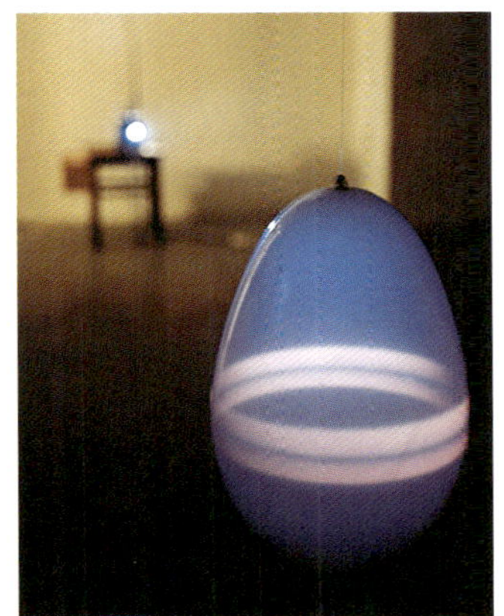

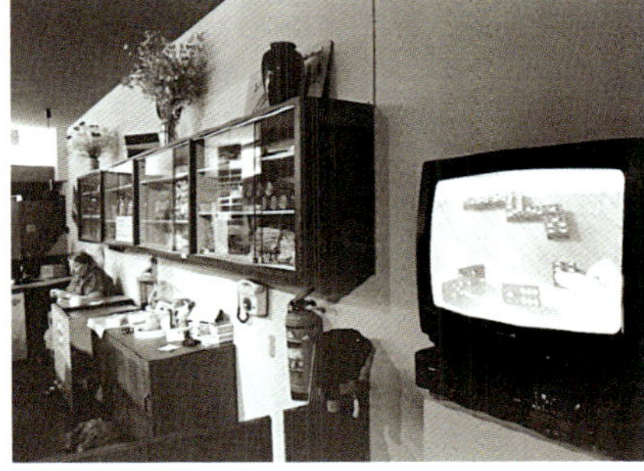

83

#5 **Jogger, 1992/93** mit Astrid S. Klein, Video, 20 Minuten, ohne Ton. Zu sehen sind Porträtaufnahmen von schwer atmenden Joggern direkt nach dem Lauf, im Zustand der Erschöpfung. *Jogger, 1992/93 with Astrid S. Klein, video, 20 minutes, no sound. Portraits of joggers breathing heavily in a state of exhaustion directly after running.*

#6 **Blumen-Vase, 1993** Polyesterform, Diapositiv, Projektor, Holz, 169 x 100 x 110 cm. Zugrunde liegt das Foto einer kleinen funktionslosen Vase (ohne Öffnung), die in eine mannshohe Polyesterform übertragen wurde. Es gibt eine Tag- und eine Nachtansicht. Bei Nacht wird auf die Form, die wie eine Attrappe durch ein Gerüst gestützt wird, ein Dia projiziert. *Flower Vase, 1993 polyester form, slide, projector, wood, 169 x 100 x 110 cm. This is based on the photograph of a small non-functional vase (no opening), which was recast into a head-high polyester shape. There is a day and a night view. At night, a slide is projected onto the shape, which is supported by props like a dummy.*

#7 **Paravent, 1994** Video (50 Minuten), Videobeamer, Diapositive, Diaprojektor, Papiertüte und Glühbirne auf einem Drehmotor, chinesische Tonfigur, zwei Bambus-/Eisengestelle mit paraventförmigen Projektionsflächen, circa 165 x 210 x 250 cm. Videoprojektion, Diaprojektion und vom Drehmotor bewegte Schattenbilder überlagern sich. Die Apparatur mit ihren projizierten Bild- und Videosequenzen erzeugt eine Atmosphäre ›bemühter Annäherung an Asien‹. *Folding Screen, 1994 video (50 minutes), video beamer, slides, slide projector, paper bag and light bulb on a rotary motor, Chinese clay figure, two bamboo/iron racks with screen-like projection surfaces, ca. 165 x 210 x 250 cm. Video projections, slide projections and moving shadowgraphs from the rotary motor are superimposed. The contraption with its projected picture and video sequences evokes the atmosphere of a ›laboured approach to Asia‹.*

#5

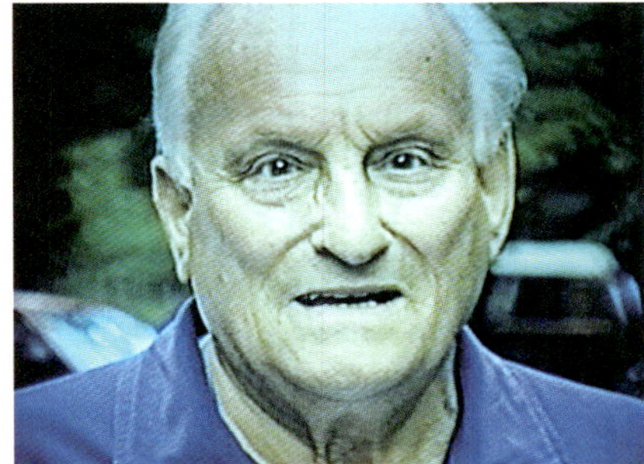

#6

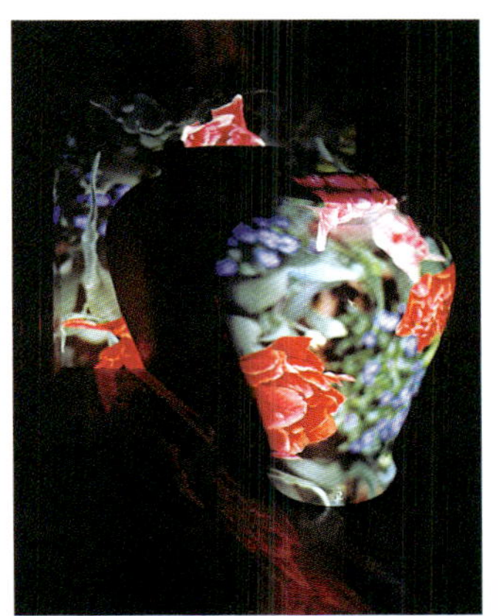 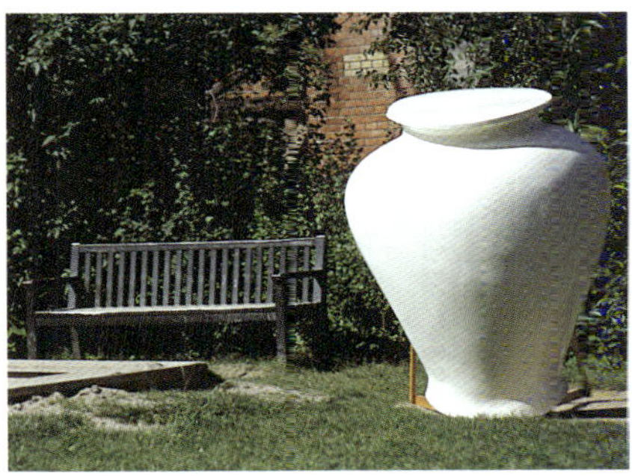

#7

85

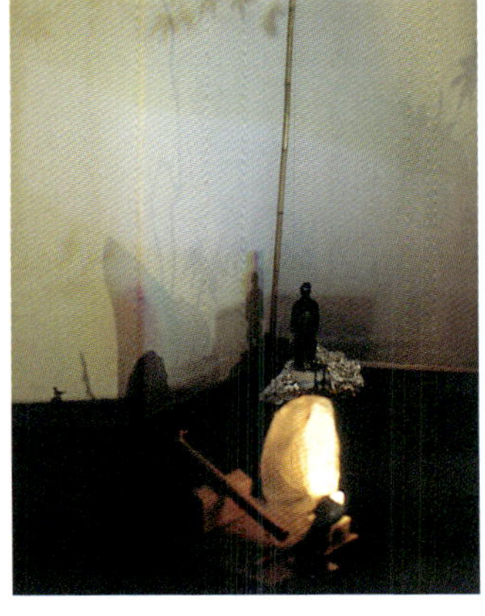 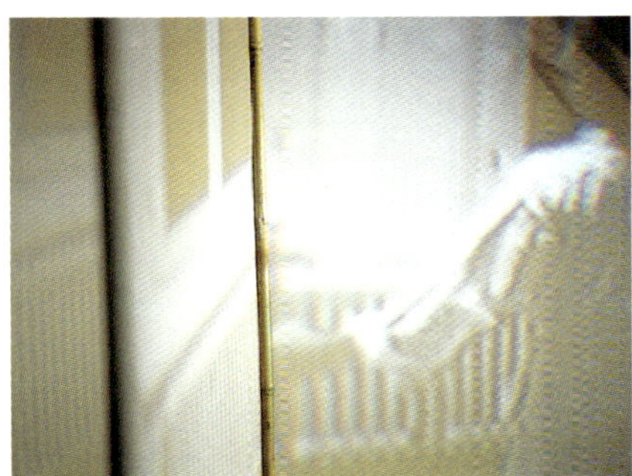

#8 **Das Fischchen, 1993-95** Kunststoff mit Sinusprofil, Drehmotor mit Diaprojektor und Glühbirne, Ventilator, Topfpflanze, 169 x 250 x 50 cm. In einem kurzen Abschnitt der halbtransparenten Form schlängelt sich regelmäßig ein projizierter roter Fisch entlang. Der Ventilator bringt die Pflanze zu einem leichten Zittern. *Little Fish, 1993-95 plastic with sinus profile, rotary motor with slide projector and light bulb, ventilator, potted plant, 169 x 250 x 50 cm. A projected red fish continuously undulates along a short sector of the semi-transparent shape. The fan makes the plant tremble slightly.*

#9 **Lady, 1995** Eisengestell, mit Charmeuse bespannt, Glühlampe, 270 x 110 x 110 cm. Über einem großen Korpus hängen zwei kleinere korbartige Formen. In einem der Körbe blinkt eine roséfarbene Glühlampe in unregelmäßigem Rhythmus. *Lady, 1995 iron frame covered with tricot fabric, light bulb, 270 x 110 x 110 cm. Two smaller basket-like shapes are draped over a large corpus. In one of the baskets a pink light bulb flashes irregularly.*

#10 **Eiger, Mönch, Jungfrau, 1996** Styropor, Glasvitrine, Nähnadeln, Faden (Multiple), 20 x 6 x 16,5 cm. *The Alpine Peaks Eiger, Mönch, Jungfrau, 1996 Styrofoam, glass showcase, needles, thread (multiple), 20 x 6 x 16.5 cm.*

#11 **Last View Manhattan, 1996** Vitrine aus Kathedralglas, Holz, Plastikfolien, Drehmotor, der ein Flugzeug aus Alufolie um zwei Schaumgummiquader führt, Schrift seitenverkehrt und auf dem Kopf: ›Manhatten im Abendlicht vom East River aus gesehen‹, 88 x 88 x 115 cm. *Last View Manhattan, 1996 showcase made from cathedral glass, wood, plastic foil, rotary motor driving an aluminium foil airplane around two foam rubber square blocks, the writing appears backwards and upside down: ›Manhattan in the evening light seen from the East River‹, 88 x 88 x 115 cm.*

#8

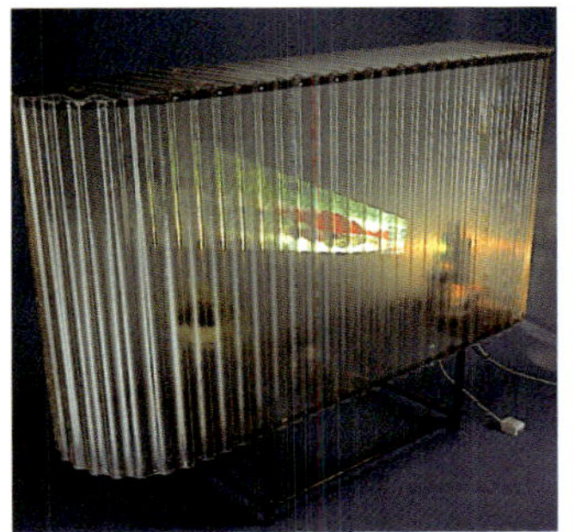 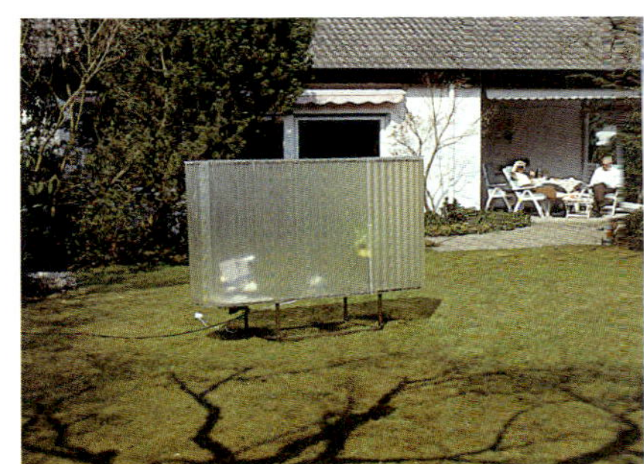

#9, #10

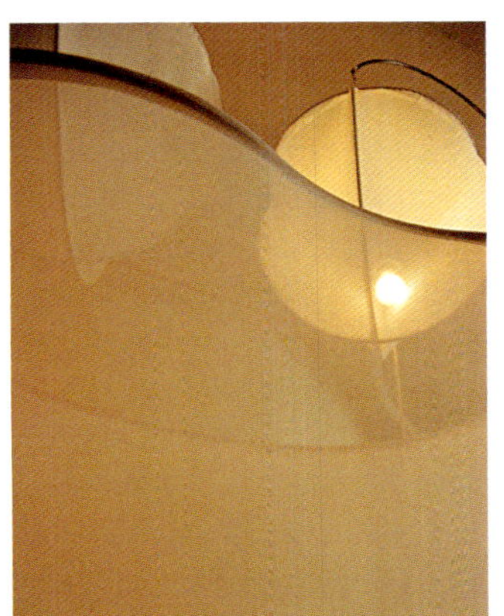 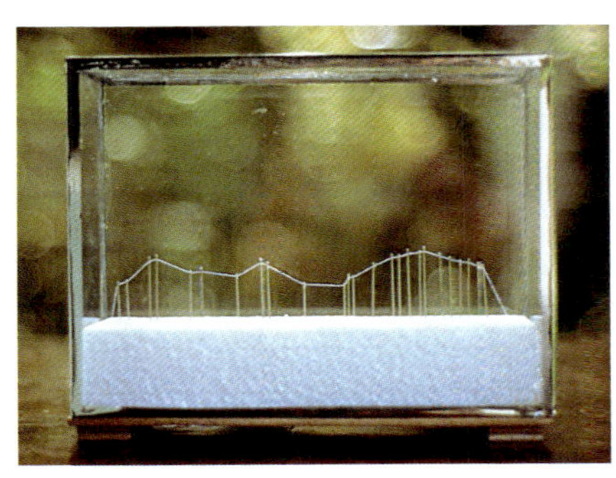

#11

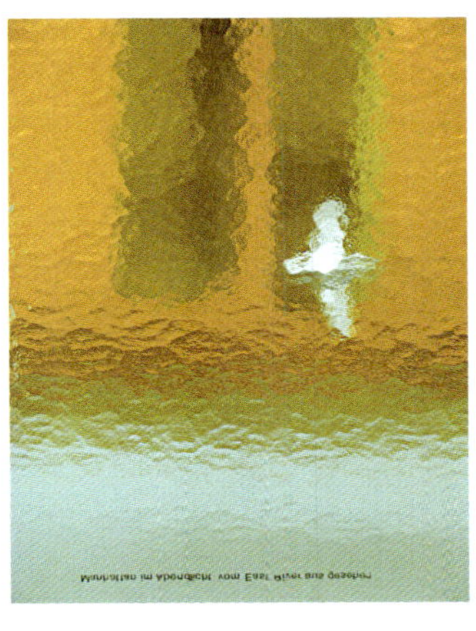
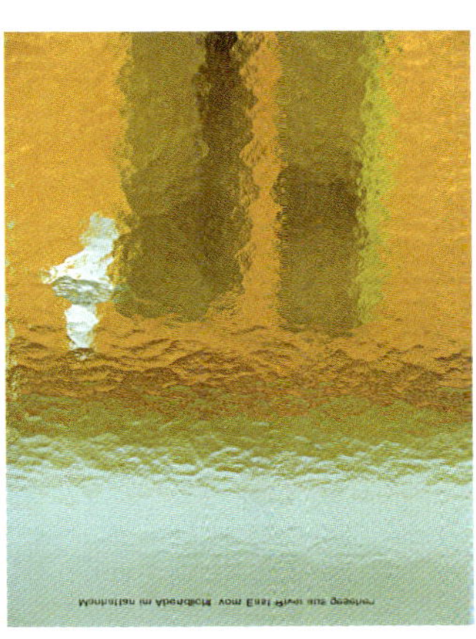

87

#12 Anmerkung zu: Langeweile, 1996 Spiegelschale, Drehmotor, Draht, Federn, Löffel, Holzplatte, Beton, 60 x 60 x 50 cm. Eine verspiegelte Halbkugel rotiert auf einem Drehmotor. Über dieser ›Schüssel‹ hängt ein Löffel an einem Draht, der kreisförmig über Betonplatten scharrt. Kleine Federn bilden die Verbindung zwischen Löffel und Draht; der Löffel stößt immer wieder mit seinem virtuellen Gegenbild zusammen. *Note to: Boredom, 1996 mirrored hemisphere, rotary motor, wire, springs, spoon, slab of wood, concrete, 60 x 60 x 50 cm. A mirrored hemisphere is turning on a rotary motor. Above the ›dish‹, a spoon is suspended from a wire that is scratching circles onto concrete slabs. Spoon and wire are joined by small springs; the spoon repeatedly collides with its virtual counterpart.*

#13 B. geht in sich – Denkmal für Michail Bakunin, 1995/96 Luftballon, Pumpe, Super-8-Film mit Endlosschleife, Küchenstuhl, Holzbrett, 42 x 54 x 96 cm (hier in einer Bibliothek mit Rechtsliteratur). Michail Bakunin (1814-1876) war ein Zeitgenosse und Kontrahent von Karl Marx und einer der Begründer des Anarchismus. Die Apparatur besteht aus einem Filmprojektor, an dessen verlängertem Objektiv sich ein Anschluss für die bereitgestellte Luftpumpe und eine Vorrichtung zum Anbringen eines Luftballons befinden. Der Betrachter muss das Gerät einschalten und den Ballon aufpumpen. In ihn wird ein Film hineinprojiziert. Das gezeigte Bild vergrößert sich und gewinnt Schärfe mit dem Volumen des Luftballons. Zerplatzt er, muss ein neuer über das Objektiv gestülpt werden. Der blau-schwarze Film zeigt Bakunin, der mit nach innen gekehrtem Blick und pathetischer Geste erscheint. *B. Soul-searching – Monument to Michail Bakunin, 1995/96 balloon, pump, Super-8-film with infinite loop, kitchen chair, wooden board, 42 x 54 x 96 cm (here in a library with legal texts). Michail Bakunin (1814-1876), contemporary and opponent of Karl Marx, was a founder of anarchism. The apparatus consists of a film projector whose extended lens features an air pump connection and a contraption for fastening a balloon. The viewer is expected to turn on the device and inflate the balloon, into which a film is being projected. The picture becomes larger and more defined as the volume of the balloon increases. If the balloon bursts a new one must be fastened to the lens. The blue-and-black film shows Bakunin looking withdrawn and with a pathetic gesture.*

12

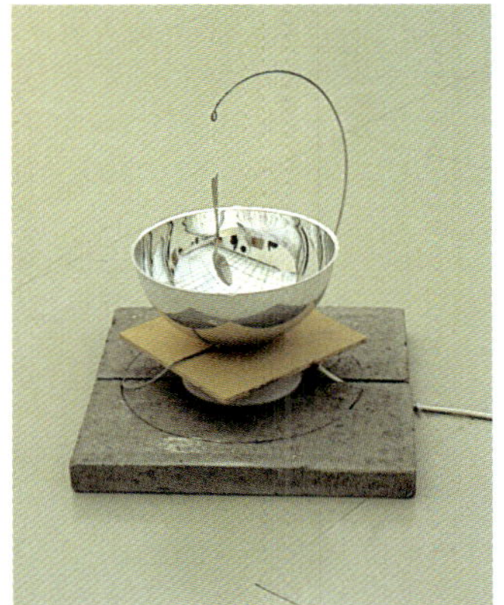

13

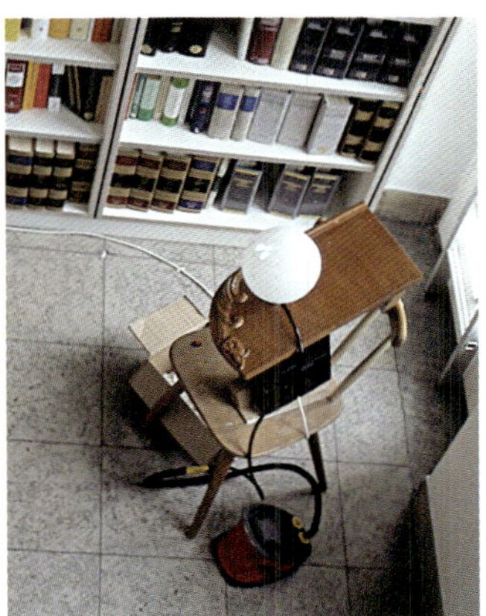

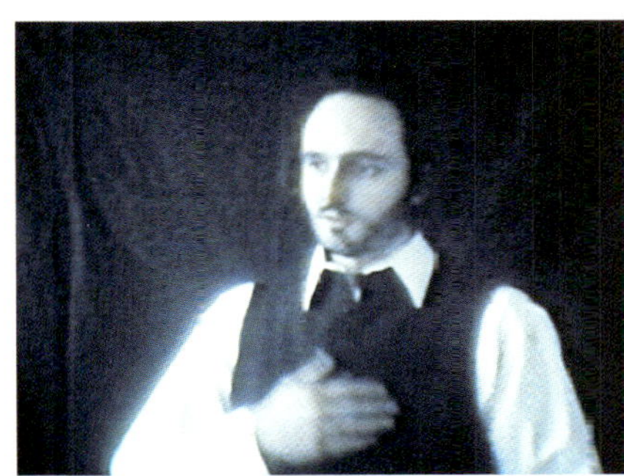

#14 **Manche haben Pech. Gegenstand zum Thema Landschafts-architektur, 1996** Holzböcke, Glasscheiben, Knetgummi, 120 x 72 x 75 cm *Some Have Bad Luck, Object to the Topic of Landscaping, 1996* sawhorses, sheet glass, plasticine, 120 x 72 x 75 cm.

#15 **Tageslichtstrecke, 1997** Siebdruck auf Glas, Spiegel, MDF (Multiple), 35,5 x 15,5 x 5 cm. *Stretch of Daylight, 1997* silk screen print on glass, mirror, MDF (multiple), 35.5 x 15.5 x 5 cm.

#16 **Keine Macht vertraut, 1997** Glasvitrine, Gummiring mit Buchstaben, Knetgummi, 60 x 30 x 30 cm. *No Power Known, 1997* glass showcase, sealing ring with letters, plasticine, 60 x 30 x 30 cm.

#17 **Die Tapferkeit oder das Stärkersein als man selbst (Nr.2), 1997** Frauen-Motorradjacke, Netz, Nylonstrumpfhosen, Muschel, Metall-platte, Knete, Paketkleber, 100 x 60 x 25 cm, hier neben Gerichtsroben und einer Arbeit von Gerrit Hoogerbeets an der Garderobe einer Anwaltskanzlei. *Braveness or Being Stronger than Oneself (No.2), 1997* woman's motorcycle jacket, net, nylon pantyhose, shell, metal sheet, play dough, packaging tape, 100 x 60 x 25 cm, here next to legal gowns and a work by Gerrit Hoogerbeets at the cloakroom of a solicitor's office.

#18 **Mobiler Meister Service, 1997** Turnschuhe, Ball, 50 x 25 x 25 cm (hier auf einem Schreibtisch). Im Hintergrund: **Zwei linke Haken, 1999** linke Boxhandschuhe, Seidentuch, Holz, 60 x 40 cm. *Mobile Master Service, 1997* ball, 50 x 25 x 25 cm (here on a desk). In the backgrond: *Two Left Hooks, 1999* left-hand boxing gloves, silk cloth, wood, 60 x 40 cm.

#14

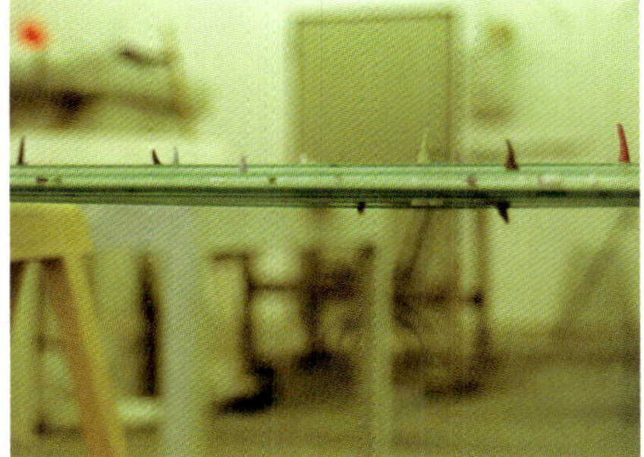

#15, #16

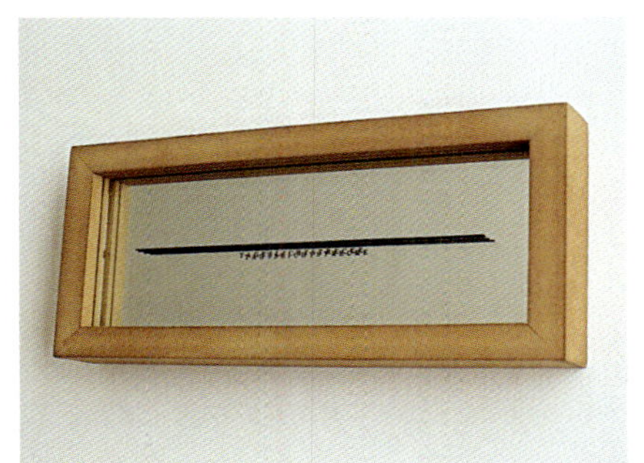
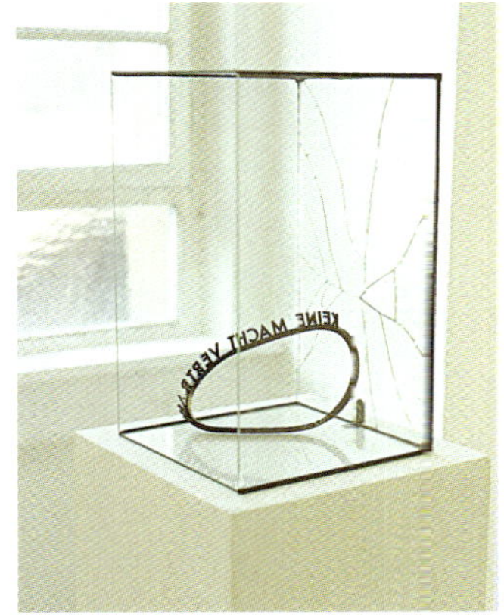

#17, #18

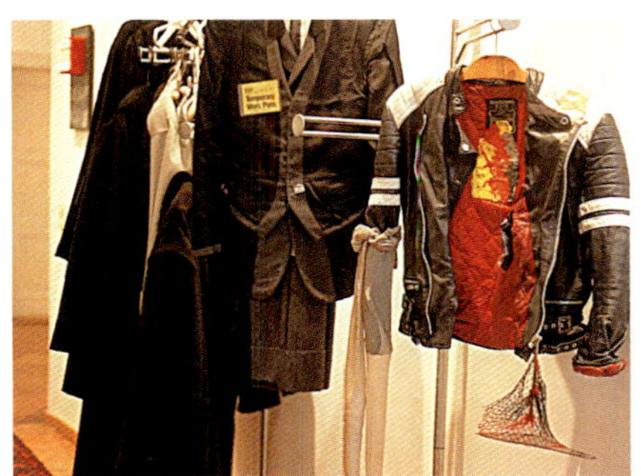
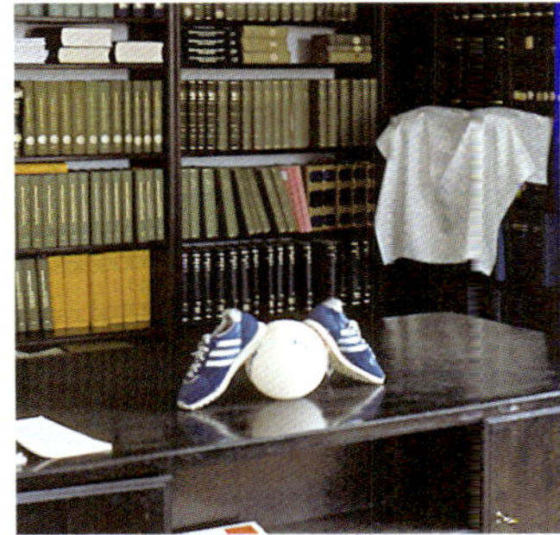

ULRIKE FLAIG

1962	geboren in Esslingen
seit 1982	Studium der Kunstgeschichte, Literaturwissenschaft und Bildhauerei in Paris, Regensburg und Stuttgart; längere Studien und Auslandsaufenthalte in Florenz, New York, China, Hamburg und Berlin
seit 1999	Ausstellungen und Projekte mit Lichtinstallationen, Bewegung, Projektion und Video; Künstlerische Zusammenarbeit mit Musikern und dem Komponisten Jim Franklin, Sydney
1993	Erster Preis des 11. Bundeswettbewerbs des Bundesministeriums für Bildung und Wissenschaft
1994	Arbeitsstipendium der Kunststiftung Baden-Württemberg
1994	Arbeitsstipendium der Kunstfonds e.V., Bonn
seit 1997	Lehraufträge an der Hochschule für Gestaltung, Technik und Wissenschaft, Pforzheim, und am Institut für Kunstgeschichte der Universität Stuttgart
2000	Sybille-Assmus-Preis, Heidelberger Kunstverein

1962	*born at Esslingen*
since 1982	*studies in art history, literature and sculpture in Paris, Regensburg and Stuttgart; extended stays in Florence, New York, China, Hamburg and Berlin for study and work purposes*
since 1990	*exhibitions and projects featuring works that include light installations, movement, projections and video; joint projects with musicians and the composer Jim Franklin, Sydney*
1993	*winner of the 11. Bundeswettbewerb des Bundesministeriums für Bildung und Wissenschaft (national competition sponsored by the Ministry for Education and Science)*
1994	*working grant from the art foundation Kunststiftung Baden-Württemberg*
1994	*working grant from the organization Kunstfonds e.V., Bonn*
since 1997	*lectureships at the university Hochschule für Gestaltung, Technik und Wirtschaft at Pforzheim and the Institut für Kunstgeschichte (Institute for Art History) at the University of Stuttgart*
2000	*Sybille-Assmus-Award, Heidelberger Kunstverein*

AUSSTELLUNGEN AUSWAHL *EXHIBITIONS SELECTION*

1995 **BANDITS – MAGES 95** Bourges, 4èmes rencontres européennes et mondiales d'ar vidéo

BEGREIFUNGSKRÄFTE – KÜNSTLERINNEN HEUTE Badischer Kunstverein e V.,
Karlsruhe und Ulm

1996 **ARTIFIZIELLE NATUR** Städtische Galerie Böblingen

DENKMAL FÜR MICHAIL BAKUNIN Neue Gesellschaft für Bildende Kunst, Berli
und / *and* Mundaneum A.S.B.L., Mons, Belgien

GULLIVERS REISEN Württembergischer Kunstverein, Stuttgart

1997 **SEOUL – DIALOG – HAMBURG** K3 auf Kampnagel, Hamburg

1998 **ANMERKUNGEN ZU: LANGEWEILE** Kunstverein Baselland, Kunsthaus Muttenz, Basel
(Einzelausstellung *Solo Exhibition*)

1999 **EUROPE IN THE BOX** ACC-Galerie Weimar, Prag, Sofia etc.

SOUNDCHECK Gesellschaft der Freunde junger Kunst e. V., Baden-Baden
(Einzelausstellung *Solo Exhibition*)

2000 **Bahnwärterhaus** Galerie der Stadt Esslingen Villa Merkel, Esslingen
(Einzelausstellung *Solo Exhibition*)

2001 **Heidelberger Kunstverein** (in Vorbereitung *in Preparation*)

BIBLIOGRAFIE AUSWAHL *BIBLIOGRAPHY SELECTION*

RENATE WIEHAGER, SE SOUVENIR – (SE) DESILLUSIONNER – (SE) PROJETER ODER REKON-
STRUKTION – KONSTRUKTION – PROJEKTION. ZU DEN ARBEITEN VON ULRIKE FLAIG, in: Kunststiftung
Baden-Württemberg (Hrsg.), Mediale Welten, Galerie der Stadt Sindelfingen, Stuttgart 1997

EVA-MARINA FROITZHEIM, ULRIKE FLAIG – METAMORPHOSEN ODER DIE KUNST DER
OBERFLÄCHE, in: Zeitung des Kunstvereins Baselland, Nr. 1, Muttenz 1998

MARTIN SCHICK, BRUDERKUSS, in: ACC-Galerie Weimar (Hrsg.), Europe in the Box,
Weimar 1999

Diese Publikation erscheint anlässlich der Ausstellung ›Soundcheck‹ bei der Gesellschaft der Freunde Junger Kunst e.V. in Baden-Baden 1999 und in der Galerie der Stadt Esslingen, Bahnwärterhaus 2000. *This catalogue is published on the occasion of the exhibition ›Soundcheck‹ at the Gesellschaft der Freunde Junger Kunst e.V. art society at Baden-Baden in 1999 and at the Esslingen Municipal Gallery, Bahnwärterhaus, in 2000.*

Herausgeber *Editor* Renate Wiehager, Galerie der Stadt Esslingen, Bahnwärterhaus; Gesellschaft der Freunde Junger Kunst Baden-Baden e.V.

Verlagslektorat *Copy editing* Judith Vajda (deutsch), Claudia Spinner (engl.)

Übersetzungen *Translations* Claudia Spinner, Jim Franklin

Grafische Gestaltung *Graphic Design* Margarethe Schmiedel, Berlin

Herstellung *Production* Peter Krecek

Satz *Typesetting* Margarethe Schmiedel

Reproduktion *Reproduction* Fotosatz Weyhing-digital, Ostfildern-Ruit

Gesamtherstellung *Printed by* Dr. Cantz'sche Druckerei, Ostfildern-Ruit

© 2000 Hatje Cantz Verlag, Ulrike Flaig und Autoren *and authors*

© 2000 für die abgebildeten Werke bei der Künstlerin *for the reproduced works by the artist*

Erschienen im *Published by* Hatje Cantz Verlag, Senefelderstraße 12, D-73760 Ostfildern-Ruit, Telefon: 00 49/7 11/4 40 50 Fax: 00 49/7 11/4 40 52 20, Internet: www.hatjecantz.de

Distribution in the US D.A.P., Distributed Art Publishers, Inc. 155 Avenue of the Americas, Second Floor, USA-New York, N.Y. 10013-1507 Tel. 0 01/2 12/6 27 19 99, Fax 0 01/2 12/6 27 94 84

ISBN 3-7757-9026-8

Printed in Germany

Fotonachweis *Photo Credits* Ulrike Flaig, außer den folgenden *except for:* Serge Hasenböhler: 38; Ingo Pompe: 87; Martin Schick: 76-77; die arge lola, Andreas Langen, Kai Loges, Stuttgart: 12-13, 30-31, 41, 45, 48-49, 83 #2 #5 #6

Umschlagabbildung *Cover illustration* Ulrike Flaig, Im Hof *in the Courtyard*

Ich bedanke mich herzlich bei Claudia Stein von Photography now, Berlin, Jim Franklin, Sydney, und Frank Roitzsch für ihre Unterstützung. Ulrike Flaig *I would like to thank Claudia Stein of Photography now, Berlin, Jim Franklin, Sydney, and Frank Roitzsch for their generous support.* Ulrike Flaig

Mit freundlicher Unterstützung von *With the kind support of* Stiftung Landesbank Baden-Württemberg und *and* Ritter Sport

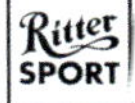